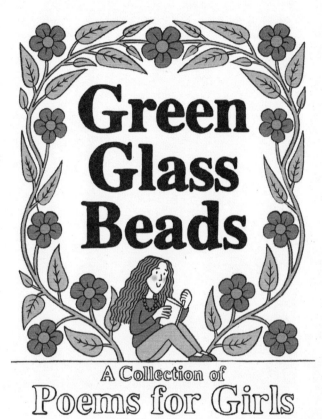

Green Glass Beads

A Collection of

Poems for Girls

First published 2011 by Macmillan Children's Books
a division of Macmillan Publishers Limited
20 New Wharf Road, London N1 9RR
Basingstoke and Oxford
Associated companies throughout the world
www.panmacmillan.com

ISBN 978-0-230-75815-5

1 3 5 7 9 8 6 4 2

A CIP catalogue record for this book is available from
the British Library.

Printed and bound in the UK by CPI Mackays, Chatham ME5 8TD

Jacqueline Wilson

Green Glass Beads

A Collection of

Poems for Girls

MACMILLAN CHILDREN'S BOOKS

Contents

Foreword by Jacqueline Wilson   xxiii

Friends

Me & You	Mandy Coe	2
Tunbridge Wells	Fleur Adcock	4
Friends	Elizabeth Jennings	5
Sporty People	Wendy Cope	6
Prior Knowledge	Carol Ann Duffy	7
Sassenachs	Jackie Kay	8
When My Friend Anita Runs	Grace Nichols	10
It Is a Puzzle	Allan Ahlberg	11
Summer Romance	Jackie Kay	13
I'm Nobody! Who Are You?	Emily Dickinson	14
Give Yourself a Hug	Grace Nichols	15

Family

Sleep, Baby, Sleep	Anon.	18
New Baby	Jackie Kay	19
My Baby Brother's Secrets	John Foster	20
Balloons	Sylvia Plath	21
Sister in a Whale	Julie O'Callaghan	23
Human Affection	Stevie Smith	24
The Housemaid's Letter	Clare Bevan	25
Sidcup, 1940	Fleur Adcock	27
Sensing Mother	Mandy Coe	28
Daddy Fell into the Pond	Alfred Noyes	29
Aunt Jennifer's Tigers	Adrienne Rich	30
Uncle and Auntie	John Hegley	31
Uncle Edward's Affliction	Vernon Scannell	32
Granny Granny Please Comb My Hair	Grace Nichols	33

Grandmamma's Birthday	Hilaire Belloc	34
Indifference	Harry Graham	35
Your Grandmother	Carol Ann Duffy	36
Rooty Tooty	Carol Ann Duffy	38
Grandpa's Soup	Jackie Kay	40

Nymphs, Mermaids, Fairies, Witches – and One Giantess

Overheard on a Saltmarsh	Harold Monro	42
from Prothalamion	Edmund Spenser	44
Sabrina Fair	John Milton	45
The Mermaid	Alfred, Lord Tennyson	46
The Merman	Alfred, Lord Tennyson	47
Wish	Mandy Coe	48
The Girl Who Could See Fairies	Marian Swinger	49
The Spider	Clare Bevan	50
A Fairy Went a-Marketing	Rose Fyleman	51
I'd Love to Be a Fairy's Child	Robert Graves	53
The Fairy's Song	William Shakespeare	54
The Fairies	William Allingham	55
Thrice Toss These Oaken Ashes in the Air	Thomas Campion	57
The Old Witch in the Copse	Frances Cornford	58
Fire, Burn; and Cauldron, Bubble	William Shakespeare	60
The Giantess	Carol Ann Duffy	61

Clothes

My Sari	Debjani Chatterjee	64
Patchwork	Adèle Geras	65
My Hat	Stevie Smith	66
Purple Shoes	Irene Rawnsley	67
Red Boots On	Kit Wright	69
Warning	Jenny Joseph	71

Birds and Animals

The Prayer of the Little Ducks — Carmen Bernos de Gasztold, translated from the French by Rumer Godden — 74

A Melancholy Lay — Marjory Fleming — 75

The Swallow — Christina Rossetti — 76

The Owl and the Pussy-Cat — Edward Lear — 77

The Frog Who Dreamed She Was an Opera Singer — Jackie Kay — 79

The Singing Cat — Stevie Smith — 80

The Song of the Jellicles — T. S. Elliot — 81

The Cat and the Moon — W. B. Yeats — 83

Diamond Cut Diamond — Ewart Milne — 84

My Cat Jeoffry — Christopher Smart — 85

The Tyger — William Blake — 87

A Sonnet on a Monkey — Marjory Fleming — 88

The Cow — Robert Louis Stevenson — 89

Cow — Ted Hughes — 90

The Blessing — James Wright — 91

A Small Dragon — Brian Patten — 92

Toy Dog — Carol Ann Duffy — 93

A Garden of Bears — U. A. Fanthorpe — 94

Animals — Sharon Thesen — 96

School

Halfway Street, Sidcup — Fleur Adcock — 98

St Gertrude's, Sidcup — Fleur Adcock — 99

A Poetry on Geometry — Ruhee Parelkar — 100

Inside Sir's Matchbox — John Foster — 102

Dream Team — Frances Nagle — 104

Make It Bigger, Eileen! — Joseph Coelho — 106

The New Girl — Clare Bevan — 107

Mrs Mackenzie — Gillian Floyd — 109

The Day After — Wes Magee — 110

Squirrels and Motorbikes	David Whitehead	113
The Fairy School under the Loch	John Rice	114
We Lost Our Teacher to the Sea	David Harmer	115
Ms Fleur	Mary Green	117
Changed	Dave Calder	119
Teacher	Carol Ann Duffy	120
St Judas Welcomes Author Philip Arder	Philip Ardagh	121

Birth and Death

You're	Sylvia Plath	126
Morning Song	Sylvia Plath	127
Drury Goodbyes	Fleur Adcock	128
Not Waving but Drowning	Stevie Smith	129
Song	Christina Rossetti	130
Remember	Christina Rossetti	131
Fidele's Dirge	William Shakespeare	132
Stop All the Clocks,	W. H. Auden	133
Break, Break, Break	Alfred, Lord Tennyson	134
Ariel's Song	William Shakespeare	135
The Stranger	Walter de la Mare	136

Children

A Song about Myself	John Keats	138
What Are Little Girls ...	Adrian Henri	140
The Boy Actor	Noel Coward	142
The Adventures of Isabel	Ogden Nash	145
maggie and milly and molly and may	E. E. Cummings	148
Equestrienne	Rachel Field	149
Brendon Gallacher	Jackie Kay	150
If No One Ever Marries Me	Laurence Alma-Tadema	152
Colouring In	Jan Dean	153

Amanda!	Robin Klein	154
Halo	Carol Ann Duffy	156
Good Girls	Irene Rawnsley	158

Women
Minnie and Winnie	Alfred, Lord Tennyson	160
Tarantella	Hilaire Belloc	161
Unwilling Country Life	Alexander Pope	163
Annabel-Emily	Charles Causley	164
The Ice	Wilfrid Gibson	166
The History of Sixteen Wonderful Old Women	Anon.	167

Love
The Janitor's Boy	Nathalia Crane	172
Romance	Robert Louis Stevenson	173
Expecting Visitors	Jenny Joseph	174
Love Hearts	Michaela Morgan	175
The Twelve Days of Christmas	Anon.	177
Dear True Love	U. A. Fanthorpe	181
Party	Adrian Henri	182
Indoor Games near Newbury	John Betjeman	183
A Birthday	Christina Rossetti	186
from The Princess	Alfred, Lord Tennyson	187
The Passionate Shepherd to His Love	Christopher Marlowe	188
Love You More	James Carter	189
How Do I Love Thee?	Elizabeth Barrett Browning	190
Sally in our Alley	Henry Carey	191
Renouncement	Alice Meynell	194
A Quoi Bon Dire	Charlotte Mew	195
As I Walked Out One Evening	W. H. Auden	196
Sonnet 18	William Shakespeare	199

Stories

La Belle Dame Sans Merci | John Keats | 202
The Song of Wandering Aengus | W. B. Yeats | 204
The Jumblies | Edward Lear | 205
On St Catherine's Day | Charles Causley | 208
The Lady of Shalott | Alfred, Lord Tennyson | 210

Fruit and Flowers

This Is Just to Say | William Carlos Williams | 218
from The Old Wives' Tale | George Peele | 219
Given an Apple | Elizabeth Jennings | 220
Moonlit Apples | John Drinkwater | 221
Millions of Strawberries | Genevieve Taggard | 222
from Goblin Market | Christina Rossetti | 223
What Is Pink? | Christina Rossetti | 225
Time of Roses | Thomas Hood | 226
Lilies Are White | Anon. | 227
Daffodils | William Wordsworth | 228
Foxgloves | Ted Hughes | 229
Spring Song | William Shakespeare | 230
Loveliest of Trees | A. E. Housman | 231
Come On into My Tropical Garden | Grace Nichols | 232
Time | Mary Ursula Bethell | 233

Places

I Remember, I Remember | Thomas Hood | 236
Cottage | Eleanor Farjeon | 238
The Lake Isle of Innisfree | W. B. Yeats | 239
Stopping by Woods on a Snowy Evening | Robert Frost | 240
The Way through the Woods | Rudyard Kipling | 241
Adlestrop | Edward Thomas | 242
The Counties | Carol Ann Duffy | 243

Rainbows, Moons and Stars

Spell to Bring a Smile	John Agard	246
My Heart Leaps Up	William Wordsworth	247
Above the Dock	T. E. Hulme	248
Lemon Moon	Beverly McLoughland	249
The Moon Landing	James Carter	250
Where Am I?	Wendy Cope	252
The Heavenly City	Stevie Smith	253
The More Loving One	W. H. Auden	254
When I Heard the Learn'd Astronomer	Walt Whitman	255

Index of First Lines	257
Index of Poets	263
Acknowledgements	267

Foreword

There was a craze for children's talent competitions when I was a little girl. My mum was very keen for me to take part, though I was an agonizingly shy child, who simply wanted to curl up in an armchair and read a book. I didn't possess any obvious talents. I couldn't sing in tune. I couldn't manage so much as 'Chopsticks' on the piano. I had never had ballet or tap lessons so I couldn't dance. However, as I said, I loved reading, so I was given a poetry book, encouraged to learn a long poem, and then told to recite it on stage. I was taught to speak slowly and clearly and do appropriate gestures, while wearing my party frock. A shiver of horror runs through me now at the very thought. However, the one wondrous thing about this terrible ordeal was that I learned many poems. Some of them I'd sooner forget. They weren't poems at all; they were twee rhymes. I was encouraged to lisp dreadful verses, like:

I'm sitting on the doorstep
And I'm eating bread and jam
And I isn't crying really
Though it feels as if I am.

Things perked up a little when I was given an A. A. Milne collection, though I still try hard to block out the memory of reciting 'The King's Breakfast' at the end of Clacton Pier when I'd drunk several glasses of water and then was too shy to tell the talent-contest manager I was desperate to go to the loo.

Somehow my mum still felt I needed to be encouraged, and she sent me to elocution lessons. Suddenly I found myself

learning *real* poems, taught by a retired teacher with a passion for Shakespeare. I learned chunks of *A Midsummer Night's Dream* and *As You Like It* when I was seven or so. I doubt I understood one word in ten, but I loved the sound of the language, the rhythm of the lines, the singing of the words inside my head. I realized you didn't always have to know precisely what was going on to like a poem.

I've included several Shakespeare poems in this anthology, and some quite challenging poetry – but don't worry if you can't always understand everything straight away. Sometimes you have to read a poem many times to tease out every single meaning. But there are lots and lots of fun, easy poems too that you can gulp down happily in one bite. In fact, I like to think this anthology is like a very good restaurant. It's got a very large menu, and every dish is carefully prepared and presented as beautifully as possible. You'll hopefully love some things, like many, and maybe wrinkle your nose at a few.

The joy for me is that it's *my* anthology, and I love every single poem in this book. I think my favourite is probably 'Overheard on a Saltmarsh' by Harold Monro. I first heard it at school in Year Four. Up till then I'd thought most poems had to have a particular pattern, mostly verses of four lines. I didn't know you could have a poem that was a conversation between two people – and interesting magical people at that, a nymph and a goblin. The nymph has some green glass beads, and the goblin desperately wants them. I totally understood. I've always loved jewellery (I'm the woman who often wears a ring on every finger and has bangles clanking all the way up her arm). I *saw* those green glass beads glittering in my mind's eye. I ached to possess them too. I muttered *green glass beads* on my way to

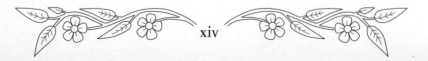

school, as if they were a magic spell.

I like magical poems and there are plenty in this book, including several that really *are* magic spells. I love poems about mermaids and fairies and witches – and I've included a wonderfully strange poem about a giantess by one of my favourite modern writers, the Poet Laureate Carol Ann Duffy. There are lots of women poets in this book because this is a special anthology for girls – but many male poets are included too.

There are also three child poets. Ruhee Parelkar wrote a poem about geometry when she was six, Nathalia Crane wrote a love poem about the janitor's boy when she was nine and I've included two poems by the wondrous little Marjory Fleming, who wrote fantastic but sometimes unintentionally funny poetry in the early nineteenth century, when she was very little. I especially like her 'Sonnet on a Monkey', which starts:

> *O lovely O most charming pug*
> *Thy graceful air and heavenly mug*

And finishes:

> *His noses cast is of the roman*
> *He is a very pretty weoman*
> *I could not get a rhyme for roman*
> *And was obliged to call it weoman.*

I think we've all had that trouble, trying to write a poem. I'm not very good at writing poems myself, though I wrote a great many when I was a teenager. But there are some poems that I feel I *might* have written, if only I had talent enough. One poem that really speaks to me – and to millions of others – is 'Warning' by

Jenny Joseph, with its famous starting lines: 'When I am an old woman I shall wear purple/With a red hat.'

It has inspired special shops that only sell purple items and a society for ladies of a certain age who visit art galleries and museums and theatres wearing purple with outrageous red hats. I was once lucky enough to meet Jenny Joseph in a bookshop, and I couldn't help being a little disappointed to see that though she *is* an old woman now she was dressed in elegant tasteful *beige*.

The 'Clothes' section of this anthology is a short but special one – the longest sections are 'Family' and 'Birds and Animals'. I've tried to choose a great variety of creatures, both real and imaginary – but there are six cat poems. I'm sorry, I just love cats. I have two: Jacob, who is grey and white and utterly gorgeous, and Thomas, who is black and slinky with enormous green eyes.

There are some very short poems and also a couple of very *long* poems. My English teacher at secondary school, Miss Pierce, read us the whole of 'The Lady of Shalott' and I was utterly enchanted and set about learning it by heart (though I can only manage a couple of verses now). I found 'Goblin Market' in a little crimson leather-bound book in my grandma's cupboard, tucked behind her sewing basket and her box of toffees. I loved this weird story of the goblins and their fruit, and clearly so did she, because when she was dying she asked if it could be buried with her. But she had a mysterious little smile on her face. She didn't usually like poetry at all, so perhaps the little book had been given to her by a long-ago sweetheart.

There's a satisfyingly thick section of love poetry in the anthology. That's the wonderful thing about poetry – you can nearly always find a poem to chime with a particular mood. If

you're feeling very sad and sorry for yourself, it's just the time to read melancholy poems. If you're feeling fond of your friends and family, there are selections to make you smile. If you're fed up with your baby brother yelling or your mum nagging at you, then you'll find poems that echo your feelings. If you're feeling very lonely, then Emily Dickinson and Grace Nichols will be comforting.

I've tried hard to include some funny poems too. I think *my* favourite funny poem is Philip Ardagh's piece about a dreadful school visit. I guarantee it will make any children's author shriek with laughter. Teachers come in all shapes and sizes, as I've shown in my 'School' section. I do hope you have a teacher who really loves poetry and chats to you about it and reads it aloud beautifully (*not* in a special strange sing-song voice). If so, you'll probably love poetry too. But if not, and you think most poetry is silly rubbish that you can't understand, please give the poems in the book a chance. Maybe try reading them aloud to yourself. They're all my special favourites, but they won't necessarily be yours too. Read as many anthologies as you can – and then maybe write and tell me *your* favourites.

Jacqueline Wilson

FRIENDS

Me & You

The long-legged girl who takes goal-kicks
is me,
I loop my 'j' and 'g's.
twiddle my hair
and wobbled a loose tooth
through History all yesterday afternoon.

The small shy boy who draws dragons
is you.
You can multiply,
make delicious cheese scones
and when my tooth finally
falls out and I cry in surprise,
you hand me a crumpled tissue.

I will be an Olympic athlete,
Win two bronze medals.
You will be a vet with gentle hands
Who gets cats to purr and budgies speak.

We don't know this yet
but we will be each other's first date.
One kiss.
That's all ... but
for the rest of our lives we never, ever forget.

In the meantime,
my tongue explores the toothless gap
and you lean over your desk and concentrate
on drawing the feathery,
feathery lines of a dragon's wings.

Mandy Coe

Tunbridge Wells

My turn for Audrey Pomegranate,
all-purpose friend for newcomers;
the rest had had enough of her –
her too-much hair, her too-much flesh,
her moles, her sideways-gliding mouth,
her smirking knowledge about rabbits.

Better a gluey friend than none,
and who was I to pick and choose?
She nearly stuck; but just in time
I met a girl called Mary Button,
a neat Dutch doll as clean as soap,
and Audrey P. was back on offer.

Fleur Adcock

Friends

I fear it's very wrong of me
And yet I must admit,
When someone offers friendship
I want the *whole* of it.
I don't want everybody else
To share my friends with me.
At least, I want *one* special one,
Who indisputedly,

Likes me much more than all the rest,
Who's always on my side,
Who never cares what others say,
Who lets me come and hide
Within his shadow; in his house –
It doesn't matter where –
Who lets me simply be myself,
Who's always, *always* there.

Elizabeth Jennings

Sporty People

I took her for my kind of person
And it was something of a shock
When my new friend revealed
That, once upon a time,
She was a Junior County Tennis Champion.

How could that happen?
How could I accidentally
Make friends with a tennis champion?
How could a tennis champion
Make friends with me?

She wasn't stupid. She read books.
She had never been mean to me
For being bad at games.
I decided to forgive
Her unfortunate past.

Sporty people can be OK –
Of course they can.
Later on, I met poets
Who played football. It's still hard
To get my head round that.

Wendy Cope

Prior Knowledge

Prior Knowledge was a strange boy.
He had sad green eyes.
He always seemed to know when I was telling lies.

We were friends for a summer.
Prior got out his knife
and mixed our bloods so we'd be brothers for life.

You'll be rich, he said, and famous;
but I must die.
Then brave, clever Prior began to cry.

He knew so much.
He knew the day before
I'd drop a jam jar full of frogspawn on the kitchen floor.

He knew there were wasps
in the gardening gloves.
He knew the name of the girl I'd grow up to love.

The day he died
he knew there would be
a wind shaking conkers from the horse chestnut tree;

and an aimless child
singing down Prior's street,
with bright red sandals on her skipping feet.

Carol Ann Duffy

Sassenachs

Me and my best pal (well, she was
till a minute ago) are off to London.
First trip on an intercity alone.
When we got on we were the same
kind of excited – jigging on our seats,
staring at everyone. But then,
I remembered I had to be sophisticated.
So when Jenny started shouting,
'Look at that, the land's flat already,'
when we were just outside Glasgow
(Motherwell actually) I'd feel myself flush.
Or even worse, 'Sassenach country!
Wey Hey Hey.' The tartan tammy
sitting proudly on top of her pony;
the tartan scarf swinging like a tail.
The nose pressed to the window.
'England's not so beautiful, is it?'
And we haven't even crossed the border!
And the train's jazzy beat joins her:
Sassenachs Sassenachs here we come.
Sassenachs Sassenachs Rum Tum Tum
Sassenachs Sassenachs How do you do.
Sassenachs Sassenachs WE'LL GET YOU.

Then she loses momentum, so out come
the egg mayonnaise sandwiches and
the big bottle of Bru. 'My ma's done us proud,'
says Jenny, digging in, munching loud.
The whole train is an egg and I'm inside it.
I try to remain calm; Jenny starts it again,
Sassenachs Sassenachs Rum Tum Tum.

Finally we get there: London, Euston;
and the first person on the platform
gets asked – 'Are you a genuine Sassenach?'
I want to die, but instead I say, *'Jenny!'*
He replies in that English way –
'I beg your pardon,' and Jenny screams
'Did you hear that Voice?'
And we both die laughing, clutching
our stomachs at Euston.

Jackie Kay

When My Friend Anita Runs

When my friend Anita runs
she runs straight into the headalong –
legs flashing over grass, daisies, mounds.

When my friend Anita runs
she sticks out her chest like an Olympic
champion – face all serious concentration.

And you'll never catch her looking around,
until she flies into the invisible tape
that says, she's won.

Then she turns to give me
this big grin and hug

O to be able to run like Anita,
        run like Anita,
Who runs like a cheetah.
If only, just for once, I could beat her.

Grace Nichols

10

It Is a Puzzle

My friend
Is not my friend any more.
She has secrets from me
And goes about with Tracy Hackett.

I would
Like to get her back,
Only do not want to say so.
So I pretend
To have secrets from her
And go about with Alice Banks.

But what bothers me is,
Maybe *she* is pretending
And would like *me* back,
Only does not want to say so.

In which case
Maybe it bothers her
That *I* am pretending.

But if we are both pretending,
Then really we are friends
And do not know it.

On the other hand,
How can we be friends
And have secrets from each other
And go about with other people?

My friend
Is not my friend any more,
Unless she is pretending.
I cannot think what to do.
It is a puzzle.

Allan Ahlberg

Summer Romance

I was best friends with Sabah
the whole long summer;
I admired her handwriting,
the way she smiled into
the summer evening,
her voice, melted butter.
The way her chin shone
under a buttercup.
Everyone let Sabah
go first in a long
hot summer queue.
The way she always looked
fancy, the way
she said 'Fandango',
and plucked her banjo;
her big purple bangle
banged at her wrist;
her face lit by the angle
poise lamp in her room,
her hair all a tangle,
damp from the summer heat,
Sabah's eyes sparkled all summer.
But when the summer was gone
and the winter came,
in walked Big Heather Murphy.
Sabah turned her lovely head
towards her. I nearly died.
Summer holidays burn with lies.

Jackie Kay

13

I'm Nobody! Who Are You?

I'm nobody! Who are you?
Are you nobody, too?
Then there's a pair of us – don't tell!
They'd banish us, you know.

How dreary to be somebody!
How public, like a frog
To tell your name the livelong day
To an admiring bog!

Emily Dickinson

Give Yourself a Hug

Give yourself a hug
when you feel unloved

Give yourself a hug
when people put on airs
to make you feel a bug

Give yourself a hug
when everyone seems to give you
a cold-shoulder shrug

Give yourself a hug –
a big big hug

And keep on singing,
'Only one in a million like me
Only one in a million-billion-trillion-zillion
like me.'

Grace Nichols

FAMILY

Sleep, Baby, Sleep

Sleep, baby, sleep
Your father tends the sheep
Your mother shakes the dreamland tree
And from it fall sweet dreams for thee
Sleep, baby, sleep

Anon.

New Baby

My baby brother makes so much noise
that the Rottweiler next door
phoned up to complain.

My baby brother makes so much noise
that all the big green frogs
came out the drains.

My baby brother makes so much noise
that the rats and the mice
wore headphones.

My baby brother makes so much noise
that I can't ask my mum a question,
so much noise that sometimes

I think of sitting the cat on top of him
in his pretty little cot with all his teddies.
But even the cat is terrified of his cries.

So I have devised a plan. A soundproof room.
A telephone to talk to my mum.
A small lift to receive food and toys.

Thing is, it will cost a fortune.
The other thing is, the frogs have gone.
It's not bad now. Not that I like him or anything.

Jackie Kay

My Baby Brother's Secrets

When my baby brother
wants to tell me a secret,
he comes right up close.
But instead of putting his lips
against my ear,
he presses his ear
tightly against my ear.
Then, he whispers so softly
that I can't hear
a word he is saying.

My baby brother's secrets
are safe with me.

John Foster

Balloons

Since Christmas they have lived with us,
Guileless and clear,
Oval soul-animals,
Taking up half the space,
Moving and rubbing on the silk

Invisible air drifts,
Giving a shriek and pop
When attacked, then scooting to rest, barely trembling.
Yellow cathead, blue fish –
Such queer moons we live with

Instead of dead furniture!
Straw mats, white walls
And these travelling
Globes of thin air, red, green,
Delighting

The heart like wishes or free
Peacocks blessing
Old ground with a feather
Beaten in starry metals.
Your small

Brother is making
His balloon squeak like a cat.
Seeming to see
A funny pink world he might eat on the other side of it,
He bites,

Then sits
Back, fat jug
Contemplating a world clear as water,
A red
Shred in his little fist.

Sylvia Plath

Sister in a Whale

You live in the hollow of a stranded whale
lying on top of our house.
My father was embarrassed by this
so a roof was put up as camouflage.
On the ribs you have hung plants
and a miniature replica of a whale
to remind you where you are.
The stomach lining is plastered with posters
and your *Snoopy for President* buttons
are stuck to a piece of blubber beside your bed.
Through the spout you observe cloud formations.
It isn't as orderly as a regular room:
its more like a shipwreck of notebooks,
school projects, shirts, paper bags,
coke cans, photographs and magazines
that has been washed up with the tide.
You beachcomb every morning for something to wear;
then it's down the corkscrew
to the real world.

Julie O'Callaghan

Human Affection

Mother, I love you so.
Said the child, I love you more than I know.
She laid her head on her mother's arm,
And the love between them kept them warm.

Stevie Smith

The Housemaid's Letter

Dear Mum,
> My life is very fine here
> Far from the village
> And the smells of home.

> I have a room in the roof
> Painted blue as a blackbird's egg,
> And a whole bed to myself,
> Which is lonely
> But so clean
> The sheets crackle like morning frost.

And I have tried
Truly
To make you proud of me, Mum.
I work hard all day,
Cleaning and polishing this great house
Till it sparkles as brightly
As a butterfly's wing.
Then I disappear down the Servants' Stair
Like a small, sweaty
Fairy Godmother,
Unseen and unknown
By the golden ones above. ➤

And I am happy enough, Mum.
The food is good
Though swallowed in silence.
The other girls smile
At my clumsy ways
And Cook can be kind
If the milk is sweet
And the butter cool.

But sometimes,
When the Sunday bells are ringing,
I still miss the warmth of the little ones
Curled beside me in the tumbled darkness,
And I hunger to hear
The homely peal
Of your lost laughter,
Mum.

Clare Bevan

Sidcup, 1940

I was writing my doll's name on the back of her neck
when Mummy caught fire – a noisy distraction.

She was wearing a loose blue flowered smock
(an old maternity smock, I now deduce,

from her pregnancy with my sister four years earlier,
being used as an overall, not to waste it);

the hem flapped over the hearth she was sweeping,
and caught on a live coal from last night's fire.

I tore myself away from writing 'Margaret'
to save her life. 'Lie down, Mummy!' I said,

and helped to smother her flames in the hearthrug.
So much is memory. The rest was praise:

What a good girl, how sensible, how calm!
But 'how well-taught' is what they should have said.

She saved her own life, really. She'd made sure
we knew fire travels upwards, and needs air.

After all, this was the 'phoney war' –
she was waiting for all of England to catch fire.

Fleur Adcock

Sensing Mother

Dad keeps Mum's favourite dress
deep in the bottom of the ottoman.
Sometimes, when he is at work
I stand listening to the tick of the clock
then go upstairs.

And propping up
the squeaky wooden lid, I dig through
layers of rough, winter blankets
feeling for that touch of silk.
The blue whisper of it cool
against my cheek.

Other times – the school-test times,
and Dad-gets-home-too-late-
to-say-goodnight times –
I wrap the arms of the dress around me,
breathing in a smell, faint as dried flowers.

I remember how she twirled around
– like a swirl of sky.

When I am old enough I will wear it.
Pulling up the white zip,
I'll laugh and spin,
calling out to my daughter:
How do I look?

Mandy Coe

Daddy Fell into the Pond

Everyone grumbled. The sky was grey.
We had nothing to do and nothing to say.
We were nearing the end of a dismal day.
And there seemed to be nothing beyond,
    Then
        Daddy fell into the pond!

And everyone's face grew merry and bright,
And Timothy danced for sheer delight.
'Give me the camera, quick, oh quick!
He's crawling out of the duckweed!' Click!

Then the gardener suddenly slapped his knee,
And doubled up, shaking silently,
And the ducks all quacked as if they were daft,
And it sounded as if the old drake laughed.
Oh, there wasn't a thing that didn't respond
    When
        Daddy fell into the pond!

Alfred Noyes

Aunt Jennifer's Tigers

Aunt Jennifer's tigers prance across a screen,
Bright topaz denizens of a world of green.
They do not fear the men beneath the tree;
They pace in sleek chivalric certainty.

Aunt Jennifer's fingers fluttering through her wool
Find even the ivory needle hard to pull.
The massive weight of Uncle's wedding band
Sits heavily upon Aunt Jennifer's hand.

When Aunt is dead, her terrified hands will lie
Still ringed with ordeals she was mastered by.
The tigers in the panel that she made
Will go on prancing, proud and unafraid.

Adrienne Rich

Uncle and Auntie

my auntie gives me a colouring book and crayons
I begin to colour
after a while auntie leans over and says
you've gone over the lines
what do you think they're there for
eh?
some kind of statement is it?
going to be a rebel are we?
your auntie gives you a lovely present
and you have to go and ruin it
I begin to cry
my uncle gives me a hanky and some blank paper
do some doggies of your own he says
I begin to colour
when I have done
he looks over
and says they are all very good
he is lying
only some of them are

John Hegley

Uncle Edward's Affliction

Uncle Edward was colour-blind;
We grew accustomed to the fact.
When he asked someone to hand him
The green book from the window seat
And we observed its bright red cover
Either apathy or tact
Stifled comment. We passed it over.
Much later, I began to wonder
What a curious world he wandered in,
Down streets where pea-green pillar boxes
Grinned at a fire engine as green;
How Uncle Edward's sky at dawn
And sunset flooded marshy green.
Did he ken John Peel with his coat so green
And Robin Hood in Lincoln red?
On country walks avoid being stung
By nettles hot as a witch's tongue?
What meals he savoured with his eyes:
Green strawberries and fresh red peas,
Green beef and greener burgundy.
All unscientific, so it seems:
His world was not at all like that,
So those who claim to know have said.
Yet, I believe, in war-smashed France
He must have crawled from neutral mud
To lie in pastures dark and red
And seen, appalled, on every blade
The rain of innocent green blood.

Vernon Scannell

32

Granny Granny Please Comb My Hair

Granny Granny please comb my hair
you always take your time
you always take such care

You put me on a cushion between your knees
you rub a little coconut oil
parting gentle as a breeze

Mummy Mummy
she's always in a hurry-hurry
rush
she pulls my hair
sometimes she tugs

But Granny
you have all the time
in the world
and when you're finished
you always turn my head and say
'Now who's a nice girl?'

Grace Nichols

Grandmamma's Birthday

Dear Grandmamma, with what we give,
We humbly pray that you may live
For many, many happy years:
Although you bore us all to tears.

Hilaire Belloc

34

Indifference

When Grandmamma fell off the boat,
And couldn't swim (and wouldn't float),
Matilda just stood by and smiled.
I almost could have slapped the child.

Harry Graham

Your Grandmother

Remember, remember, there's many a thing
your grandmother doesn't dig
if it ain't got that swing;
many a piece of swag
she won't pick up and put in her bag
if it seems like a drag.
She painted it red – the town –
she lassooed the moon.
Remember, remember, your grandmother
boogied on down.

Remember, remember, although your grandmother's old,
she shook, she rattled, she rolled.
She was so cool she was cold,
she was solid gold.
Your grandmother played it neat,
wore two little blue suede shoes
on her dancing feet –
oo, reet-a-teet-teet –
Remember, remember, your grandmother
got with the beat.

Remember, remember, it ain't what you do
it's the way that you do it.
Your grandmother knew it –
she had a balloon and she blew it,
she had a ball
and was belle of it
just for the hell of it.
She was Queen of the night.
Remember, remember, your grandmother's
aaaaaaaaaaaalllllll riiiiiiiiiiiight.

Carol Ann Duffy

Rooty Tooty

Grandad used to be a pop star,
with a red-and-silver guitar.
He wore leather jackets and drainpipe jeans.
He drove around in limousines,
waving to screaming fans.
Fab! said Grandad. *Groovy!*
I really dig it, man!

Grandad used to have real hips,
he swivelled and did The Twist.
His record went to Number One.
Grandad went like this:
Rooty tooty, yeah yeah.
Rooty tooty, yeah yeah.
Rooty tooty, yeah yeah.
Then Grandad met Gran.

Gran was dancing under a glitterball.
Grandad was on bass.
He noticed how a thousand stars
sparkled and shone in her face.
And although Gran fancied the drummer,
Grandad persevered. He wrote Gran
a hundred love songs
down through their happy years.

Grandad used to be a pop star,
a rock'n'roll man –
Rooty tooty, yeah yeah yeah –
and Grandad loved groovy Gran,

Carol Ann Duffy

Grandpa's Soup

No one makes soup like my Grandpa's,
with its diced carrots the perfect size
and its diced potatoes the perfect size
and its wee soft bits –
what are their names? –
and its big bit of hough,
which rhymes with loch, floating
like a rich island in the middle of the soup sea.

I say. Grandpa, Grandpa, your soup is the
    best soup in the whole world.
And Grandpa says, Och,
which rhymes with hough and loch,
Och, don't be daft,
because he's shy about his soup, my Grandpa.
He knows I will grow up and pine for it.
I will fall ill and desperately need it.
I will long for it my whole life after he is gone.
Every soup will become sad and wrong after
    he is gone.
He knows when I'm older I will avoid soup altogether.
Oh Grandpa, Grandpa, why is your soup so glorious? I say,
tucking into my fourth bowl in a day.

Barley! That's the name of the wee soft bits. Barley.

Jackie Kay

NYMPHS, MERMAIDS, FAIRIES, WITCHES – AND ONE GIANTESS

Overheard on a Saltmarsh

Nymph, nymph, what are your beads?

Green glass, goblin. Why do you stare at them?

Give them me.

        No.

Give them me. Give them me.

            No.

Then I will howl all night in the reeds,
Lie in the mud and howl for them.

Goblin, why do you love them so?

They are better than stars or water,
Better than voices of winds that sing,
Better than any man's fair daughter,
Your green glass beads on a silver ring.

Hush, I stole them out of the moon.

Give me your beads, I want them.

No.

I will howl in a deep lagoon
For your green glass beads. I love them so
Give them me. Give them.

No

Harold Monro

43

from Prothalamion

There, in a meadow, by the river's side,
A flock of nymphs I chanced to espy,
All lovely daughters of the flood thereby,
With goodly greenish locks all loose untied,
As each had been a bride;
And each one had a little wicker basket,
Made of fine twigs entrailèd curiously,
In which they gathered flowers to fill their flasket,
And with fine fingers cropped full feateously
The tender stalks on high.
Of every sort, which in that meadow grew,
They gathered some, the violet pallid blue,
The little daisy that at evening closes,
The virgin lily, and the primrose true,
With store of vermeil roses,
To deck their bridegrooms' posies,
Against the bridal day, which was not long:
    Sweet Thames, run softly, till I end my song.

Edmund Spenser

Sabrina Fair

Sabrina fair
    Listen where thou art sitting
Under the glassy, cool, translucent wave,
    In twisted braids of Lillies knitting
The loose train of thy amber-dropping hair,
    Listen for dear honour's sake,
    Goddess of the silver lake,
                Listen and save.

John Milton

The Mermaid

I

Who would be
A mermaid fair,
Singing alone,
Combing her hair
Under the sea,
In a golden curl
With a comb of pearl,
On a throne?

II

I would be a mermaid fair;
I would sing to myself the whole of the day.
With a comb of pearl I would comb my hair;
And still as I combed I would sing and say,
'Who is it loves me? who loves not me?'
I would comb my hair till my ringlets would fall
    Low adown, low adown,
And I should look like a fountain of gold
    Springing alone
    With a shrill inner sound,
    Over the throne
    In the midst of the hall.

Alfred, Lord Tennyson

46

The Merman

I
Who would be
A merman bold,
Sitting alone,
Singing alone
Under the sea,
With a crown of gold,
On a throne?

II
I would be a merman bold;
I would sit and sing the whole of the day.
I would fill the sea-halls with a voice of power
But at night I would roam abroad and play
With the mermaids in and out of the rocks,
Dressing their hair with the white sea-flower;
And holding them back by their flowing locks
I would kiss them often under the sea,
And kiss them again till they kissed me
    Laughingly, laughingly;
And then we would wander away, away,
To the pale sea-groves straight and high,
    Chasing each other merrily.

Alfred, Lord Tennyson

Wish

She wished she could fly.
She wished for friends
who were birds and flowers.
She wished she wore a silver frock.

She wished she could speak
with a magic tongue.
She wished so hard.
She wished so hard.

Now she works
in the baker's shop.
She wears a white coat
and a netted cap.

She speaks the language
of mam and dad
and at the end of each day
her feet hurt.

But at night she carries her baby
up to the stars. She sings to him
in the language of flowers.
He reaches out to touch her silver wings.

Mandy Coe

The Girl Who Could See Fairies

Wings whispered about her hair
as she walked, half in the Otherworld,
half in the mortal realm.
She saw massive oaks
dwarfing the grimy buildings,
overlaying them like great, dark ghosts.
She glimpsed, with her double vision,
a white stag leaping through the passing traffic
and felt a wreath of berries placed lightly on her head.
Bluebells burst through the pavement beneath her feet
and she trod through them as if in a dream.
Nobody believed that she could see fairies.
She was mocked
and, eventually, locked
into a hospital room
from where, one day,
she stepped out of the mortal world
and into the Otherworld,
leaving the room empty
but for the scent of forests.

Marian Swinger

The Spider

The fairy child loved her spider.

Even when it grew fat
And grey and old,
She would comb its warm fur
With a hazel twig
And take it for slow walks
On its silky lead.

Sometimes it played cat-cradles with her
But more often it wove hammocks
Among the long grasses
And they swung together under friendly trees.

When it died,
Her mother bought her a money spider
Who scuttled and tumbled to make her smile.
But it wasn't the same,
And still, when she curls up to sleep
In the lonely dawn,
She murmurs her old spider's name.

Clare Bevan

A Fairy Went a-Marketing

A fairy went a-marketing –
    She bought a little fish;
She put it in a crystal bowl
    Upon a golden dish.
An hour she sat in wonderment
    And watched its silver gleam,
And then she gently took it up
    And slipped it in a stream.

A fairy went a-marketing –
    She bought a coloured bird;
It sang the sweetest, shrillest song
    That ever she had heard.
She sat beside its painted cage
    And listened half the day,
And then she opened wide the door
    And let it fly away.

A fairy went a-marketing –
    She bought a winter gown
All stitched about with gossamer
    And lined with thistledown.
She wore it all the afternoon
    With prancing and delight,
Then gave it to a little frog
    To keep him warm at night.

A fairy went a-marketing –
     She bought a gentle mouse
To take her tiny messages,
     To keep her tiny house.
All day she kept its busy feet
     Pit-patting to and fro,
And then she kissed its silken ears,
     Thanked it, and let it go.

Rose Fyleman

I'd Love to Be a Fairy's Child

Children born of fairy stock
Never need for shirt or frock,
Never want for food or fire,
Always get their heart's desire:
Jingle pockets full of gold,
Marry when they're seven years old,
Every fairy child may keep
Two strong ponies and ten sheep;
All have houses, each his own,
Built of brick or granite stone;
They live on cherries, they run wild –
I'd love to be a fairy's child.

Robert Graves

53

The Fairy's Song

from A Midsummer Night's Dream

Over hill, over dale,
Thorough bush, thorough brier,
Over park, over pale,
Thorough flood, thorough fire,
I do wander everywhere,
Swifter than the moon's sphere;
And I serve the fairy queen,
To dew her orbs upon the green.
The cowslips tall her pensioners be;
In their gold coats spots you see;
Those be rubies, fairy favours,
In those freckles live their savours.
I must go seek some dewdrops here,
And hang a pearl in every cowslip's ear.

William Shakespeare

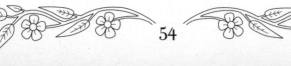

The Fairies

Up the airy mountain,
    Down the rushy glen,
We daren't go a-hunting
    For fear of little men;
Wee folk, good folk,
    Trooping all together;
Green jacket, red cap,
    And white owl's feather!

Down along the rocky shore
    Some make their home,
They live on crispy pancakes
    Of yellow tide-foam;
Some in the reeds
    Of the black mountain lake,
With frogs for their watch-dogs,
    All night awake.

High on the hill-top
    The old King sits;
He is now so old and gray
    He's nigh lost his wits.
With a bridge of white mist
    Columbkill he crosses,
On his stately journeys
    From Slieveleague to Rosses;
Or going up with music
    On cold starry nights,
To sup with the Queen
    Of the gay Northern Lights. ⟿

They stole little Bridget
    For seven years long;
When she came down again
    Her friends were all gone.
They took her lightly back,
    Between the night and morrow,
They thought that she was fast asleep,
    But she was dead with sorrow.
They have kept her ever since
    Deep within the lake,
On a bed of flag-leaves,
    Watching till she wake.

By the craggy hill-side,
    Through the mosses bare,
They have planted thorn-trees
    For pleasure here and there.
Is any man so daring
    As dig them up in spite,
He shall find their sharpest thorns
    In his bed at night.

Up the airy mountain,
    Down the rushy glen,
We daren't go a-hunting
    For fear of little men;
Wee folk, good folk,
    Trooping all together;
Green jacket, red cap,
    And white owl's feather!

William Allingham

Thrice Toss These Oaken Ashes in the Air

Thrice toss these oaken ashes in the air,
Thrice sit thou mute in this enchanted chair;
Then thrice three times tie up this true love's knot.
And murmur soft: 'She will, or she will not.'

Go burn these poisonous weeds in yon blue fire,
These screech-owl's feathers and this prickling briar,
This cypress gathered at a dead man's grave,
That all thy fears and cares an end may have.

Then come, you fairies, dance with me a round;
Melt her hard heart with your melodious sound.
In vain are all the charms I can devise;
She hath an art to break them with her eyes.

Thomas Campion

The Old Witch in the Copse

I am a witch, and a kind old witch,
    There's many a one that knows that –
Alone I live in my little dark house
    With Pillycock, my cat

A girl came running through the night
    When all the winds blew free:–
'O mother, change a young man's heart
    That will not look on me.

O mother, brew a magic mead
    To stir his heart so cold.'
'Just as you will, my dear,' said I;
    'And I thank you for your gold.'

So here am I in the wattled copse
    Where all the twigs are brown,
To find what I need, to brew my mead
    As the dark of night comes down.

Primroses in my old hands,
    Sweet to smell and young,
And violets blue that spring in the grass
    Wherever the larks have sung.

With celandines as heavenly crowns
  Yellowy-gold and bright;
All of these, O all of these,
  Shall bring her love's delight.

But orchids growing snakey-green
  Speckled dark with blood,
And fallen leaves that sered and shrank
  And rotted in the mud,

With nettles burning blistering harsh
  And blinding thorns above;
All of these, O all of these
  Shall bring the pains of love.

Shall bring the pains of love, my Puss,
  That cease not night or day,
The bitter rage, nought can assuage
  Till it bleeds the heart away.

Pillycock mine, my hands are full,
  My pot is on the fire.
Purr, my pet, this fool shall get
  Her fool's desire.

Frances Cornford

Fire, Burn; and Cauldron, Bubble

from Macbeth

Round about the cauldron go;
In the poison'd entrails throw.
Toad, that under cold stone
Days and nights has thirty-one
Swelter'd venom, sleeping got,
Boil thou first i'th'charmèd pot.
Double, double toil and trouble:
Fire, burn; and cauldron, bubble.
Fillet of a fenny snake,
In the cauldron boil and bake;
Eye of newt, and toe of frog,
Wool of bat, and tongue of dog,
Adder's fork, and blind-worm's sting,
Lizard's leg, and howlet's wing.
For a charm of powerful trouble,
Like a hell-broth boil and bubble.
Double, double toil and trouble:
Fire, burn; and cauldron, bubble.

William Shakespeare

The Giantess

Where can I find seven small girls to be pets,
where can I find them?
One to comb the long grass of my hair
with this golden rake,
one to dig with this copper spade
the dirt from under my nails.
I will pay them in crab apples.

Where can I find seven small girls to help me,
where can I find them?
A third to scrub at my tombstone teeth
with this mop in its bronze bucket,
a fourth to scoop out the wax from my ears
with this platinum trowel.
I will pay them in yellow pears.

Where can I find seven small girls to be good dears,
where can I find them?
A fifth one to clip the nails of my toes
with these sharp silver shears,
a sixth to blow my enormous nose
with this satin sheet.
I will pay them in plums. ➤

But the seventh girl will stand on the palm of my hand,
singing and dancing,
and I will love the tiny music of her voice,
her sweet little jigs.
I will pay her in grapes and kumquats and figs.
Where can I find her?
Where can I find seven small girls to be pets?

Carol Ann Duffy

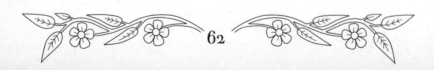

CLOTHES

My Sari

Saris hang on the washing line:
a rainbow in our neighbourhood.
This little orange one is mine,
it has a mango leaf design.
I wear it as a Rani would.
It wraps round me like sunshine,
it ripples silky down my spine,
and I stand tall and feel so good.

Debjani Chatterjee

Patchwork

She starts with red.
Everything begins with strange mixtures of blood:
vein branches under white skin, white sheets spotted scarlet,
a rose opening slowly on a green ground,
flowering over the fabric.

She takes blue for skies,
small squares of daylight in a sloping wall,
long washes of midnight ocean broken by anxious moons turning.
Blue firmaments, pale blue for the sorrow,
lapis lazuli of ancient denim.

Sometimes yellow chooses her.
Lunatic daisies grin in white bonnets,
and saffron, ochre, persimmon blaze under her scorched hands.
Soothe them with butter, comfortable primrose.
Avoid the sun. Seek shadows.

Is she superstitious about green?
She drowns in colours of water. Debatable shades: turquoise,
peacock, teal, aquamarine. Shuns emerald, lime and olive.
Sometimes grass green is a background.
She tries to look away.

She needs black everywhere:
a fence around flowers, barrier between one colour
and another. A thin reminder that through azure and crimson
our days are stitched with black and we have black
as a lining for our closed eyes.

Adèle Geras

My Hat

Mother said if I wore this hat
I should be certain to get off with the right sort of chap
Well look where I am now, on a desert island
With so far as I can see no one at all on hand
I know what has happened though I suppose Mother wouldn't
   see
This hat being so strong has completely run away with me
I had the feeling it was beginning to
   happen the moment I put it on
What a moment that was as I rose up,
   I rose up like a flying swan
As strong as a swan too, why see how
   far my hat has flown me away
It took us a night to come and then a night and a day
And all the time the swan wing in my hat waved beautifully
Ah, I thought, How this hat becomes me.
First the sea was dark but then it was pale blue
And still the wing beat and we flew and we flew
A night and a day and a night, and by the old right way
Between the sun and the moon we flew until morning day.
It is always early morning here on this peculiar island
The green grass grows into the sea on the dipping land
Am I glad I am here? Yes, well, I am,
It's nice to be rid of Father, Mother and the young man
There's just one thing causes me a twinge of pain,
If I take my hat off, shall I find myself home again?
So in this early morning land I always wear my hat
Go home, you see, well I wouldn't run a risk like that.

Stevie Smith

Purple Shoes

Mum and me had a row yesterday,
a big, exploding
howdareyouspeaktomelikethatI'mofftostayatGran's
kind of row.

It was about shoes.
I'd seen a pair of purple ones at Carter's,
heels not too high, soft suede, silver buckles;
'No,' she said.
'Not suitable for school.
I can't afford to buy rubbish.'
That's when we had our row.
I went to bed longing for those shoes.
They made footsteps in my mind,
kicking up dance dust;
I wore them in my dreams across a shiny floor,
under flashing coloured lights.
It was ruining my life not to have them. ➜

This morning they were mine.
Mum relented and gave me the money.
I walked out of the store wearing new purple shoes.
I kept seeing myself reflected in shop windows
with purple shoes on,
walking to the bus stop,
walking the whole length of our street
wearing purple shoes.

On Monday I shall go to school in purple shoes.
Mum will say no a thousand furious times
But I don't care.
I'm not going to give in.

Irene Rawnsley

Red Boots On

Way down Geneva,
All along Vine,
Deeper than the snow drift
Love's eyes shine.

Mary Lou's walking
In the winter time.

She's got

Red boots on, she's got
Red boots on,
Kicking up the winter
Till the winter's gone.

So

Go by Ontario,
Look down Main,
If you can't find Mary Lou,
Come back again.

Sweet light burning
In winter's flame.

She's got

Snow in her eyes, got
A tingle in her toes
And new red boots on
Wherever she goes

So

All around Lake Street,
Up by St Paul,
Quicker than the white wind
Love takes all.

Mary Lou's walking
In the big snow fall.

She's got

Red boots on, she's got
Red boots on,
Kicking up the winter
Till the winter's gone.

Kit Wright

Warning

When I am an old woman I shall wear purple
With a red hat which doesn't go, and doesn't suit me,
And I shall spend my pension on brandy and summer gloves
And satin sandals, and say we've no money for butter.
I shall sit down on the pavement when I'm tired
And gobble up samples in shops and press alarm bells
And run my stick along the public railings
And make up for the sobriety of my youth.
I shall go out in my slippers in the rain
And pick the flowers in other people's gardens
And learn to spit.

You can wear terrible shirts and grow more fat
And eat three pounds of sausages at a go
Or only bread and pickle for a week
And hoard pens and pencils and beermats and things in boxes.

But now we must have clothes that keep us dry
And pay the rent and not swear in the street
And set a good example for the children.
We must have friends to dinner and read the papers.
But maybe I ought to practise a little now?
So people who know me are not too shocked and surprised
When suddenly I am old and start to wear purple.

Jenny Joseph

BIRDS AND ANIMALS

The Prayer of the Little Ducks

Dear God,
give us a flood of water.
Let it rain tomorrow and always.
Give us plenty of little slugs
and other luscious things to eat.
Protect all folk who quack
and everyone who knows how to swim.
Amen.

Carmen Bernos de Gasztold,
translated from the French
by Rumer Godden

A Melancholy Lay

Three Turkeys fair their last have breathed,
And now this world forever leaved,
Their Father and their Mother too
Will sigh and weep as well as you,
Mourning for their offspring fair,
Whom they did nurse with tender care.
Indeed the rats their bones have crunch'd,
To eternity are they launch'd;
Their graceful form and pretty eyes
Their fellow fowls did not despise,
A direful death indeed they had,
That would put any parent mad,
But she was more than usual calm,
She did not give a single dam.
Here ends this melancholy lay:
Farewell poor Turkeys I must say.

Marjory Fleming

The Swallow

Fly away, fly away, over the sea,
Sun-loving swallow, for summer is done.
Come again, come again, come back to me,
Bringing the summer and bringing the sun.

Christina Rossetti

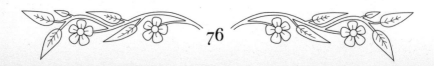

The Owl and the Pussy-Cat

The Owl and the Pussy-cat went to sea
   In a beautiful pea-green boat,
They took some honey, and plenty of money,
   Wrapped up in a five-pound note.
The Owl looked up to the stars above,
   And sang to a small guitar,
'O lovely Pussy! O Pussy, my love,
     What a beautiful Pussy you are,
       You are,
       You are!
     What a beautiful Pussy you are!'

Pussy said to the Owl, 'You elegant fowl!
   How charmingly sweet you sing!
O let us be married! too long we have tarried:
   But what shall we do for a ring?'
They sailed away, for a year and a day,
   To the land where the Bong-tree grows
And there in a wood a Piggy-wig stood
     With a ring at the end of his nose,
       His nose,
       His nose,
     With a ring at the end of his nose. ⇒

'Dear Pig, are you willing to sell for one shilling
    Your ring?' Said the Piggy, 'I will.'
So they took it away, and were married next day
    By the Turkey who lives on the hill.
They dined on mince, and slices of quince,
    Which they ate with a runcible spoon;
And hand in hand, on the edge of the sand,
        They danced by the light of the moon,
            The moon,
            The moon,
        They danced by the light of the moon.

Edward Lear

The Frog Who Dreamed She Was an Opera Singer

There once was a frog
who dreamed she was an opera singer.
She wished so hard she grew a long throat
and a beautiful polkadot green coat
and intense opera singer's eyes.
She even put on a little weight.
But she couldn't grow tall.
She just couldn't grow tall.
She leaped to the Queen Elizabeth Hall,
practising her sonata all the way.
Her voice was promising and lovely.
She couldn't wait to leapfrog on to the stage.
What a presence on the stage!
All the audience in the Queen Elizabeth Hall
gasped to see one so small sing like that.
Her voice trembled and swelled
and filled with colour.
That frog was a green prima donna.

Jackie Kay

The Singing Cat

It was a little captive cat
  Upon a crowded train
His mistress takes him from his box
  To ease his fretful pain.

She holds him tight upon her knee
  The graceful animal
And all the people look at him
  He is so beautiful.

But oh he pricks and oh he prods
  And turns upon her knee
Then lifteth up his innocent voice
  In plaintive melody.

He lifteth up his innocent voice
  He lifteth up, he singeth
And to each human countenance
  A smile of grace he bringeth.

He lifteth up his innocent paw
  Upon her breast he clingeth
And everybody cries, Behold
  The cat, the cat that singeth.

He lifteth up his innocent voice
  He lifteth up, he singeth
And all the people warm themselves
  In the love his beauty bringeth.

Stevie Smith

The Song of the Jellicles

Jellicle Cats come out tonight,
Jellicle Cats come one come all:
The Jellicle Moon is shining bright –
Jellicles come to the Jellicle Ball.

Jellicle Cats are black and white,
Jellicle Cats are rather small;
Jellicle Cats are merry and bright,
And pleasant to hear when they caterwaul.
Jellicle Cats have cheerful faces,
Jellicle Cats have bright black eyes;
They like to practise their airs and graces
And wait for the Jellicle Moon to rise.

Jellicle Cats develop slowly,
Jellicle Cats are not too big;
Jellicle Cats are roly-poly,
They know how to dance a gavotte and a jig.
Until the Jellicle Moon appears
They make their toilette and take their repose:
Jellicles wash behind their ears,
Jellicles dry between their toes.

Jellicle Cats are white and black,
Jellicle Cats are of moderate size;
Jellicles jump like a jumping-jack,
Jellicle Cats have moonlit eyes.
They're quiet enough in the morning hours,
They're quiet enough in the afternoon,
Reserving their terpsichorean powers
To dance by the light of the Jellicle Moon.

Jellicle Cats are black and white,
Jellicle Cats (as I said) are small;
If it happens to be a stormy night
They will practise a caper or two in the hall.
If it happens the sun is shining bright
You would say they had nothing to do at all:
They are resting and saving themselves to be right
For the Jellicle Moon and the Jellicle Ball.

T. S. Eliot

The Cat and the Moon

The cat went here and there
And the moon spun round like a top,
And the nearest kin of the moon,
The creeping cat, looked up.
Black Minnaloushe stared at the moon,
For, wander and wail as he would,
The pure cold light in the sky
Troubled his animal blood.
Minnaloushe runs in the grass
Lifting his delicate feet.
Do you dance, Minnaloushe, do you dance?
When two close kindred meet,
What better than call a dance?
Maybe the moon may learn,
Tired of that courtly fashion,
A new dance turn.
Minnaloushe creeps through the grass
From moonlit place to place,
The sacred moon overhead
Has taken a new phase.
Does Minnaloushe know that his pupils
Will pass from change to change,
And that from round to crescent,
From crescent to round they range?
Minnaloushe creeps through the grass
Alone, important and wise,
And lifts to the changing moon
His changing eyes.

W. B. Yeats

Diamond Cut Diamond

Two cats
One up a tree
One under the tree
The cat up a tree is he
The cat under the tree is she
The tree is witch elm, just incidentally.
He takes no notice of she, she takes no notice of he.
He stares at the woolly clouds passing, she stares at the tree.
There's been a lot written about cats, by Old Possum, Yeats and Company
But not Alfred de Musset or Lord Tennyson or Poe or anybody
Wrote about one cat under, and one cat up, a tree.
God knows why this should be left for me
Except I like cats as cats be
Especially one cat up
And one cat under
A witch elm
Tree.

Ewart Milne

My Cat Jeoffry

For I will consider my Cat Jeoffry.

For he is the servant of the Living God, duly and daily serving
him.

For at the first glance of the glory of God in the East he
worships in his way.

For this is done by wreathing his body seven times round with
elegant quickness.

For then he leaps up to catch the musk, which is the blessing
of God upon his prayer.

For he rolls upon prank to work it in.

For having done duty and received blessing he begins to
consider himself.

For this he performs in ten degrees.

For first he looks upon his fore-paws to see if they are clean.

For secondly he kicks up behind to clear away there.

For thirdly he works it upon stretch with the fore-paws
extended.

For fourthly he sharpens his paws by wood.

For fifthly he washes himself.

For sixthly he rolls upon wash.

For seventhly he fleas himself, that he may not be interrupted
upon the beat.

For eighthly he rubs himself against a post.

For ninthly he looks up for his instructions.

For tenthly he goes in quest of food.

For having consider'd God and himself he will consider his
neighbour.

For if he meets another cat he will kiss her in kindness.

For when he takes his prey he plays with it to give it chance.

For one mouse in seven escapes by his dallying.

For when his day's work is done his business more properly begins.

For he keeps the Lord's watch in the night against the adversary.

For he counteracts the powers of darkness by his electrical skin & glaring eyes.

For he counteracts the Devil, who is death, by brisking about the life.

For in his morning orisons he loves the sun and the sun loves him.

For he is of the tribe of Tiger.

For the Cherub Cat is a term of the Angel Tiger.

For he has the subtlety and hissing of a serpent, which in goodness he suppresses.

For he will not do destruction, if he is well-fed, neither will he spit without provocation.

For he purrs in thankfulness, when God tells him he's a good Cat.

For he is an instrument for the children to learn benevolence upon.

For every house is incompleat without him & a blessing is lacking in the spirit.

Christopher Smart

The Tyger

Tyger! Tyger! burning bright
In the forests of the night,
What immortal hand or eye
Could frame thy fearful symmetry?

In what distant deeps or skies
Burnt the fire of thine eyes?
On what wings dare he aspire?
What the hand dare seize the fire?

And what shoulder, and what art,
Could twist the sinews of thy heart?
And when thy heart began to beat,
What dread hand? and what dread feet?

What the hammer? what the chain?
In what furnace was thy brain?
What the anvil? what dread grasp
Dare its deadly terrors clasp?

When the stars threw down their spears,
And water'd heaven with their tears,
Did he smile his work to see?
Did he who made the Lamb make thee?

Tyger! Tyger! burning bright
In the forests of the night,
What immortal hand or eye
Dare frame thy fearful symmetry?

William Blake

A Sonnet on a Monkey

O lovely O most charming pug
Thy graceful air and heavenly mug
The beauties of his mind do shine
And every bit is shaped so fine
Your very tail is most divine
Your teeth is whiter than the snow
You are a great buck and a bow
Your eyes are of so fine a shape
More like a christians than an ape.
His cheeks is like the roses blume
Your hair is like the ravens plume
His noses cast is of the roman
He is a very pretty weoman
I could not get a rhyme for roman
And was obliged to call it weoman.

Marjory Fleming

The Cow

The friendly cow, all red and white,
I love with all my heart:
She gives me cream with all her might,
To eat with apple-tart.

She wanders lowing here and there,
And yet she cannot stray,
All in the pleasant open air,
The pleasant light of day;

And blown by all the winds that pass
And wet with all the showers,
She walks among the meadow grass
And eats the meadow flowers.

Robert Louis Stevenson

Cow

The Cow comes home swinging
Her udder and singing:

'The dirt O the dirt
It does me no hurt.

And a good splash of muck
Is a blessing of luck.

O I splosh through the mud
But the breath of my cud

Is sweeter than silk.
O I splush through manure

But my heart stays pure
As a pitcher of milk.'

Ted Hughes

The Blessing

Just off the highway to Rochester, Minnesota,
Twilight bounds softly forth on the grass.
And the eyes of those two Indian ponies
Darken with kindness.
They have come gladly out of the willows
To welcome my friend and me.
We step over the barbed wire into the pasture
Where they have been grazing all day, alone.
They ripple tensely, they can hardly contain their happiness
That we have come.
They bow shyly as wet swans. They love each other.
There is no loneliness like theirs.
At home once more,
They begin munching the young tufts of spring in the darkness.
I would like to hold the slenderer one in my arms,
For she has walked over to me
And nuzzled my left hand.
She is black and white,
Her mane falls wild on her forehead,
And the light breeze moves me to caress her long ear
That is as delicate as the skin over a girl's wrist.
Suddenly I realize
That if I stepped out of my body I would break
Into blossom.

James Wright

A Small Dragon

I've found a small dragon in the woodshed.
Think it must have come from deep inside a forest
because it's damp and green and leaves
are still reflecting in its eyes.

I fed it on many things, tried grass,
the roots of stars, hazelnut and dandelion,
but it stared up at me as if to say, I need
food you can't provide.

It made a nest among the coal,
not unlike a bird's but larger,
it's out of place here
and is quite silent.

If you believed in it I would come
hurrying to your house to let you share my wonder,
but I want instead to see
if you yourself will pass this way.

Brian Patten

Toy Dog

for Matthew Kay

When I come home from school he doesn't bark.
He doesn't fetch the stick I throw for him in Clissold Park,
or bite a burglar's ankle in the dark.
Toy dog.

When I wake up he doesn't lick my face.
He never beats me by a mile the times we have a race,
or digs a bone up from his secret place.
Toy dog.

When I say *Heel!* or *Sit!* he can't obey.
I buy a red dog-collar for him, though he will not stray,
or trip me up at soccer when I play.
Toy dog.

One day his brown glass eyes will soften, see.
One night, his nylon tail will wag when I come in for tea;
his cloth leg cock against a lamp post for a pee.
Good dog.

Carol Ann Duffy

A Garden of Bears

Fur is soft, skin isn't.
Paw is safe, hand isn't.
Two stiff forelegs, ready
To comfort, not rangy,
Unpredictable arms.
Bears don't speak. Bears are best.

Dolls are too close to us.
They can be trained to laugh,
To wet themselves, shoot from
The hip, explain about
Erogenous zones, need
Clothes, knives, hairdressers. Break.

Remember this: bears are
Brilliant. There was Sam, the
King of the dictionary,
Shambling, myopic, rude
To earls, tender with cats,
Slaves, women, the poor,
Minding their dignity.

Inside homely teddies,
Lolling in cots, lurks the
Grisly intransigent
Ursus horribilis,
Ten feet tall, solitary,
Surly, reeking of meat.

I know a lot of bears.
Most of them look just like
Other people. But there
Are risks. Abruptly bears
Can turn wiser than us
And braver. There are bears
Who rise to their full height,
Rise to the occasion.

U. A. Fanthorpe

Animals

When I come out of the bathroom
animals are waiting in the hall
and when I settle down to read
an animal comes between me
and my book and when I put on
a fancy dinner, a few animals
are under the table staring at the guests,
and when I mail a letter
or go to the Safeway there's always
an animal tagging along –
or crying left at home and when I get
home from work animals leap joyously
around my old red car so I feel like
an avatar with flowers & presents all over
her body, and when I dance around
the kitchen at night wild & feeling
lovely as Margie Gillis, the animals
try to dance too, they stagger on
back legs and open their mouths, pink
and black and fanged, and I take their paws
in my hands and bend toward them,
happy and full of love.

Sharon Thesen

SCHOOL

Halfway Street, Sidcup

'We did sums at school, Mummy –
you do them like this: look.' I showed her.

It turned out she knew already.

Fleur Adcock

St Gertrude's, Sidcup

Nuns, now: ladies in black hoods
for teachers – surely that was surprising?

It seems not. It was just England:
like houses made of brick, with stairs,

and dark skies, and Christmas coming
in winter, and there being a war on.

I was five, and unsurprisable –
except by nasty dogs, or the time

When I ran to catch the bus from school
and my knickers fell down in the snow.

Fleur Adcock

A Poetry on Geometry

There was once a line
Who was perfectly fine
Till one day she said,
'I need someone, who will be mine.'

So it went out to dine
With another line,
And when they were back
They formed an angle.

'We want to grow'
Said the lines of the angle
'Let's call a third one
And form a triangle.'

A fourth line came in
The triangle to share
And when it joined over
It was a square!

The square was happy
It walked on and on
Till another line joined
To form a pentagon.

When it saw another line
The pentagon said 'Come on'
So when the line joined
It was now a hexagon.

As more lines got added
New shapes were born
Heptagon, octagon, nonagon
And finally a decagon!

With lines and shapes and symmetry,
I made this poetry on Geometry.

Ruhee Parelkar

Inside Sir's Matchbox

Our teacher's pet
Lives in a nest of pencil-shavings
Inside a matchbox
Which he keeps
In the top drawer of his desk.
It's so tiny, he says,
You need a microscope to see it.
When we asked him what it ate,
He grinned and said,
'Nail clippings and strands of human hair –
Especially children's.'
Once, on Open Day,
He put it out on the display table,
But we weren't allowed to open the box,
Because it's allergic to light.

Our teacher says his pet's unique.
'Isn't it lonely?' we asked.
'Not with you lot around,' he said.
Once, there was an awful commotion
When it escaped
While he was opening the box
To check if it was all right.
But he managed to catch it
Before it got off his desk.

Since then, he hasn't taken it out much.
He says he thinks it's hibernating at present –
Or it could be pregnant.
If it is, he says,
There'll be enough babies
For us all to have one.

John Foster

Dream Team

My team
Will have all the people in it
Who're normally picked last.

Such as me.

When it's my turn to be chooser
I'll overlook Nick Magic-Feet-Jones
And Supersonic Simon Hughes

And I'll point at my best friend Sean
Who'll faint with surprise
And delight.

And at Robin who's always the one
Left at the end that no one chose –
Unless he's away, in which case it's guess who?

And Tim who can't see a thing
Without his glasses
I'll pick him.

And the rest of the guys that Mr Miller
Calls dead-legs but only need their chance
To show what they're made of.

We'll play in the cup final
In front of the class, the school, the town,
The world, the galaxy.

And due to the masterly leadership shown
By their captain, not forgetting
His three out-of-this-world goals,

We'll WIN.

Frances Nagle

Make It Bigger, Eileen!

In Art I drew a park
With a pond, and railings, and children playing ...
And trees with multi-coloured leaves
And mothers with pushchairs and wearing hats that jumped
And joggers running with three legs
And skaters – skating on thin ice with elephants on their backs
And pigeons playing cards on bread tables
And grass with eyes and noses
And flowers with walking sticks and headphones
And clouds that rained smells
And a sun as deep as an ocean
And stones that bled
And a rainbow with stairs.

Sir said ...
'Tut, tut, tut – bigger, Eileen, your picture must be bigger'
So I drew a duck.

Joseph Coelho

The New Girl

The new girl stood at Miss Moon's desk,
Her face pale as a drawing
On white paper,
Her lips coloured too heavily
With a too-dark crayon.

When the others shouted, 'Me! Me!'
I curled my fists,
Tried not to think of friendship,
Or whispered secrets,
Or games for two players.
But the empty seat beside me
Shimmered with need
And my loneliness dragged her like a magnet.

As she sat down
I caught the musty smell of old forests,
Noticed the threads that dangled
At her thin wrists,
The purple stitches that circled
Her swan's neck,
Yet I loved her quietness,
The way she held her pencil
Like a feather,
The swooping curves of her name,
The dreaminess of her cold eyes. ➠

At night, I still wonder
Where she sleeps,
If she sleeps,
And what Miss Moon will say
To her tattered parents
On Open Day.

Clare Bevan

Mrs Mackenzie

Mrs Mackenzie's quite stern.
She says, 'You're not here to have fun,
You're here to learn,'
When I mess about in class.

And in the corridor, if I run
When she's passing by, she shouts
'Slow down! You're not in a race!'
Or 'More haste, less speed!' –
Whatever *that* means.

I never used to like Mrs Mackenzie much.

But the other day
When my dog died
And she saw me crying
She said 'Dogs are such good friends,
Aren't they?'
And she let me stay
In the classroom with her at breaktime
When all the other children went outside
To play.

Mrs Mackenzie's OK.

Gillian Floyd

The Day After

I went to school
the day after Dad died.
Teacher knew all about it.
She put a hand on my shoulder
    and sighed.

In class things seemed much the same
although I was strangely subdued.
Breaktime was the same too,
and at lunchtime the usual crew
played up the dinner supervisors.
Fraggle was downright rude.
I joined in the football game

but volunteered to go in goal.
That meant I was left almost alone,
could think things over on my own.
For once I let the others shout
    and race and roll.

✳ ✳ ✳ ✳ ✳

First thing that afternoon,
everyone in his and her place
for silent reading,
I suddenly felt hot tears streaming
        down my face.

Salty tears splashed down
and soaked into my book's page.
Sobs heaved in my chest.
Teacher peered over her half specs
and said quietly, 'Ben, come here.'
I stood at her desk crying. At my age!
I felt like an idiot, a clown.

'Don't feel ashamed,' teacher said.
'It's only right to weep.
Here, have these tissues to keep.'
I dabbed my eyes, then looked around.
        Bowed into books, every head.

* * * * *

'Have a cold drink.
Go with James. He'll understand.'
In the boys' cloaks I drank deeply
then slowly wiped my mouth
        on the back of my hand.

Sheepishly I said, 'My dad died.'
'I know,' said James.
'We'd best get back to class. Come on.'
Walking down the corridor I thought of Dad . . . gone.
In class no one sniggered,
they were busy getting changed for games.
No one noticed I'd cried.

All day I felt sad, sad.
After school I reached my street,
clutching the tissues, dragging my feet.
Mum was there in our house
        but no Dad,

        no Dad.

Wes Magee

Squirrels and Motorbikes

Today we went out of school
Down the lane
Into the spinney
To watch squirrels

We saw lots of grey squirrels
Scuttling through the trees
Searching for nuts on the ground
Some as still as statues

We all took notes
Made sketches
And asked questions

Back in school
We drew our squirrels
Some sitting like
Silver grey coffee-pots
While others paddled acorns
Into the soft green grass
Some still listening with their tufty ears
Others with their feather-duster tails waving

Everyone drew a squirrel picture – except
George, who drew a motorbike
But then, he always does.

David Whitehead

The Fairy School under the Loch
(Sgoil a'Morghain, Barra, The Hebrides)

The wind sings its gusty song.
The bell rings its rusty ring.
The underwater fairy children
dive and swim through school gates.
They do not get wet.

The waves flick their flashing spray.
A school of fish wriggles its scaly way.
The underwater fairy children
learn their liquidy lessons.
Their reading books are always dry.

The seals straighten in a stretchy mass.
Teresa the Teacher flits and floats from class to class.
The underwater fairy children
count, play, sing and recite,
their clothes not in the least bit damp.

The rocks creak in their cracking skin.
A fairy boat drifts into a loch of time.
The underwater fairy children
lived, learned and left this life –
their salty stories now dry as their cracked wings.

John Rice

We Lost Our Teacher to the Sea

We've been at the seaside all day
collecting shells, drawing the view
doing science in the rockpools.

Our teacher went to find the sea's edge,
and stayed there, he's sitting on a rock
he won't come back.

His glasses are frosted over with salt
his beard has knotted into seaweed
his black suit is covered in limpets.

He's staring into the wild water
singing to the waves
sharing a joke with the herring gulls.

We sent out the coastguard
the lifeboat and the orange helicopter
he told them all to go away.

We're getting on the bus with our sticks of rock
our presents for Mum
and our jotters and pencils. ➥

He's still out there as we leave
arms outstretched to the pale blue sky
the tide racing towards him.

His slippery fishtail flaps
with a flick and a shimmer he's gone
back to the sea forever.

David Harmer

Ms Fleur

Though she doesn't know it,
Our teacher is a mermaid.
We built her from Skegness sand,
Me and Emily,
Sculpted a swishing tail,
Curved scales with the edge of our hands,
And arranged her driftwood hair in a spiky halo.

All day we piled the sand and patted her.

Though she didn't see it,
We wrote her name, Ms Fleur,
In our biggest letters,
Me and Emily,
Next to her blue shell belly button,
And her squidgy seaweed earrings
That popped between our fingers.

All day we piled the sand and patted her.

Though she didn't hear it,
We sang a mermaid song,
And screeched like seagulls,
Me and Emily,
As we fixed her fins,
And tiny pebble eyes,
Saw crabs scuttle across her shingle necklace.

All day we piled the sand and patted her. ⇒

Until finally the sea lapped at her fins,
Her driftwood hair, her seaweed earrings,
And she swished her fish tail,
High into the foam,
Calling,
'Katie, Emily,
It's time to go,
It's time for home,
It's time to say goodbye you know!'

Mary Green

Changed

For months he taught us, stiff-faced.
His old tweed jacket closely buttoned up,
his gestures careful and deliberate.

We didn't understand what he was teaching us.
It was as if a veil, a gauzy bandage, got between
what he was showing us and what we thought we saw.

He had the air of a gardener, fussily protective
of young seedlings, but we couldn't tell
if he was hiding something or we simply couldn't see it.

At first we noticed there were often scraps of leaves
on the floor where he had stood. Later, thin wisps
of thread like spider's web fell from his jacket.

Finally we grew to understand the work. And on that day
he opened his jacket, which to our surprise
seemed lined with patterned fabric of many shimmering hues.

Then he smiled and sighed. And with this movement
the lining rippled and instantly the room was filled
with a flickering storm of swirling butterflies.

Dave Calder

Teacher

When you teach me,
your hands bless the air
where chalk dust sparkles.

And when you talk,
the six wives of Henry VIII
stand in the room like bridesmaids,

or the Nile drifts past the classroom window,
the Pyramids baking like giant cakes
on the playing fields.

You teach with your voice,
so a tiger prowls from a poem
and pads between desks, black and gold

in the shadow and sunlight,
or the golden apples of the sun drop
from a branch in my mind's eye.

I bow my head again
to this tattered, doodled book
and learn what love is.

Carol Ann Duffy

St Judas Welcomes Author Philip Arder

Welcome to St Judas.
Because of a mix-up in timetabling
Miss Horace who was supposed to be looking after you today
has had to go on a factory field-trip
with gifted and talented and the two classes
of students who've actually read your book.
We've had to put you with a younger group
who, like me I must confess, have never heard of you,
but we did look you up on Wikipedia
and see that you like cats.

Perhaps you could tell a story with lots of actions
and they could pretend to be their favourite animals?

There's a note here from Miss H saying that
we are unable to buy any of your books for the library
because we've spent the budget for this school term.
The children won't be able
to purchase any of your books either,
following a change of rules recently agreed by the PTA.
We have arranged, however, for you to sign
lots of scraps of paper
of ever-diminishing
sizes.

And for you to give two extra talks,
seeing as how you're here.

A photographer from the local paper
has a small window in his busy schedule
so can only come halfway through your first event.
At this stage, we will have to stop proceedings
and remove from shot those children whose parents
have not given consent for them to be photographed.
It shouldn't take long.

And I should warn you that
there are certain children
unsuitable for audience participation.
We found that out the hard way.

I'm going to have to leave you here
in the staffroom for a while
while I find an alternative venue.
Mock exams in the main hall
mean that you'll probably have to give your
little talks in the dining room.
I'll ask the kitchen staff to keep the noise
of table-laying
to a minimum.

I'm afraid I'll have to nip out part-way through
your first event
to sort out a health and safety issue
but Mrs Lomax will be there throughout,

though she does have to finish
a pile of marking.
Mr Goody, our PE teacher, will be just down the corridor
and has promised to keep an ear out for the kids
if they get restless.
At that age, they're easily bored.

I'm sorry if things seem a little disorganized
but you must be used to it.
I imagine the big names don't do school visits,
do they?
Have you ever met Philip Pullman,
by the way?
His books are amazing.

Ah, there goes the bell.

Help yourself to coffee.
The mugs are in the sink . . .

Philip Ardagh

BIRTH AND DEATH

You're

Clownlike, happiest on your hands,
Feet to the stars, and moon-skulled,
Gilled like a fish. A common-sense
Thumbs-down on the dodo's mode.
Wrapped up in yourself like a spool,
Trawling your dark as owls do.
Mute as a turnip from the Fourth
Of July to All Fools' Day,
O high-riser, my little loaf.

Vague as fog and looked for like mail.
Farther off than Australia.
Bent-backed Atlas, our travelled prawn.
Snug as a bud and at home
Like a sprat in a pickle jug.
A creel of eels, all ripples.
Jumpy as a Mexican bean.
Right, like a well-done sum.
A clean slate, with your own face on.

Sylvia Plath

Morning Song

Love set you going like a fat gold watch.
The midwife slapped your footsoles, and your bald cry
Took its place among the elements.

Our voices echo, magnifying your arrival. New statue.
In a drafty museum, your nakedness
Shadows our safety. We stand round blankly as walls.

I'm no more your mother
Than the cloud that distils a mirror to reflect its own slow
Effacement at the wind's hand.

All night your moth-breath
Flickers among the flat pink roses. I wake to listen:
A far sea moves in my ear.

One cry, and I stumble from bed, cow-heavy and floral
In my Victorian nightgown.
Your mouth opens clean as a cat's. The window square

Whitens and swallows its dull stars. And now you try
Your handful of notes;
The clear vowels rise like balloons.

Sylvia Plath

Drury Goodbyes

What with getting in the way of the packing
and not being allowed to go to
the big event, Great-granny's funeral,

we found something silly to do, and did it:
we sat the new dolls on the potty
after we'd done wees in it ourselves.

Next day we were going away in a boat
so big that you could stand up in it,
they said, and it wouldn't tip over.

There was no time to dry the soggy dolls;
they were left behind – all but my Margaret,
who wouldn't bend enough to dunk her bottom.

Fleur Adcock

Not Waving but Drowning

Nobody heard him, the dead man,
But still he lay moaning:
I was much further out than you thought
And not waving but drowning.

Poor chap, he always loved larking
And now he's dead
It must have been too cold for him his heart gave way,
They said.

Oh, no no no, it was too cold always
(Still the dead one lay moaning)
I was much too far out all my life
And not waving but drowning.

Stevie Smith

Song

When I am dead, my dearest,
    Sing no sad songs for me;
Plant thou no roses at my head,
    Nor shady cypress tree:
Be the green grass above me
    With showers and dewdrops wet;
And if thou wilt, remember,
    And if thou wilt, forget.

I shall not see the shadows,
    I shall not feel the rain;
I shall not hear the nightingale
    Sing on, as if in pain:
And dreaming through the twilight
    That doth not rise nor set,
Haply I may remember,
    And haply may forget.

Christina Rossetti

Remember

Remember me when I am gone away,
    Gone far away into the silent land;
    When you can no more hold me by the hand
Nor I half turn to go yet turning stay.
Remember me when no more day by day
    You tell me of our future that you planned:
    Only remember me; you understand
It will be late to counsel then or pray.
Yet if you should forget me for a while
    And afterwards remember, do not grieve:
    For if the darkness and corruption leave
    A vestige of the thoughts that once I had,
Better by far you should forget and smile
    Than that you should remember and be sad.

Christina Rossetti

Fidele's Dirge
from Cymbeline

Fear no more the heat o' the sun,
    Nor the furious winter's rages;
Thou thy worldly task hast done,
    Home art gone, and ta'en thy wages.
Golden lads and girls all must,
    As chimney-sweepers, come to dust.

Fear no more the frown o' the great,
    Thou art past the tyrant's stroke;
Care no more to clothe and eat,
    To thee the reed is as the oak.
The sceptre, learning, physic, must
All follow this, and come to dust.

Fear no more the lightning-flash,
    Nor the all-dreaded thunder-stone;
Fear not slander, censure rash;
    Thou hast finished joy and moan.
All lovers young, all lovers must
Consign to thee, and come to dust.

No exorciser harm thee!
Nor no witchcraft charm thee!
Ghost unlaid forbear thee!
Nothing ill come near thee!
Quiet consummation have,
And renowned be thy grave!

William Shakespeare

Stop All the Clocks

Stop all the clocks, cut off the telephone,
Prevent the dog from barking with a juicy bone,
Silence the pianos and with muffled drum
Bring out the coffin, let the mourners come.

Let aeroplanes circle moaning overhead
Scribbling on the sky the message He Is Dead,
Put crêpe bows round the white necks of the public doves,
Let the traffic policemen wear black cotton gloves.

He was my North, my South, my East and West,
My working week and my Sunday rest,
My noon, my midnight, my talk, my song;
I thought that love would last for ever: I was wrong.

The stars are not wanted now: put out every one;
Pack up the moon and dismantle the sun;
Pour away the ocean and sweep up the wood.
For nothing now can ever come to any good.

W. H. Auden

Break, Break, Break

Break, break, break,
    On thy cold grey stones, O sea!
And I would that my tongue could utter
    The thoughts that arise in me.

O, well for the fisherman's boy,
    That he shouts with his sister at play!
O, well for the sailor lad,
    That he sings in his boat on the bay!

And the stately ships go on
    To their haven under the hill;
But O for the touch of a vanished hand,
    And the sound of a voice that is still!

Break, break, break,
    At the foot of thy crags, O sea!
But the tender grace of a day that is dead
    Will never come back to me.

Alfred, Lord Tennyson

Ariel's Song

from The Tempest

Full fathom five thy father lies,
    Of his bones are coral made:
Those are pearls that were his eyes,
    Nothing of him that doth fade,
But doth suffer a sea-change
Into something rich, and strange:
Sea-nymphs hourly ring his knell –
    Hark! now I hear them,
        Ding-dong bell.

William Shakespeare

The Stranger

Half-hidden in a graveyard,
    In the blackness of a yew,
Where never living creature stirs,
    Nor sunbeam pierces through,

Is a tomb-stone, green and crooked –
    Its faded legend gone –
With one rain-worn cherub's head
    To sing of the unknown.

There, when the dusk is falling,
    Silence broods so deep
It seems that every air that breathes
    Sighs from the fields of sleep.

Day breaks in heedless beauty,
    Kindling each drop of dew,
But unforsaking shadow dwells
    Beneath this lonely yew.

And, all else lost and faded,
    Only this listening head
Keeps with a strange unanswering smile
    Its secret with the dead.

Walter de la Mare

CHILDREN

A Song about Myself

There was a naughty boy,
  A naughty boy was he,
He would not stop at home,
  He could not quiet be –
    He took
    In his knapsack
    A book
    Full of vowels
    And a shirt
    With some towels –
    A slight cap
    For a night-cap –
    A hair brush,
    Comb ditto,
    New stockings,
    For old ones
    Would split O!
    This knapsack
    Tight at's back
    He rivetted close
And followed his nose
    To the North,
    To the North,
And followed his nose
    To the North.

There was a naughty boy,
   And a naughty boy was he,
He ran away to Scotland
   The people for to see –
      There he found
      That the ground
      Was as hard,
      That a yard
      Was as long,
      That a song
      Was as merry,
      That a cherry
      Was as red,
      That lead
      Was as weighty,
      That fourscore
      Was as eighty,
      That a door
      Was as wooden
      As in England –
So he stood in his shoes
   And he wondered,
   He wondered,
He stood in his shoes
   And he wondered.

John Keats

What Are Little Girls . . .

I'm not
a
sugar and spice
girl
an all-things-nice
girl
a do-as-told
good-as-gold
pretty frock
never shock
girl

I'm
a
slugs and snails
girl
a puppy-dogs'-tails
girl
a climbing trees
dirty knees
hole-in-sock
love-to-shock
girl

cricket bats
and big white rats
crested newts
and football boots

that's what
this little girl's

... Made Of.

Adrian Henri

The Boy Actor

I can remember. I can remember.
The months of November and December
    Were filled for me with peculiar joys
So different from those of other boys
    For other boys would be counting the days
Until end of term and holiday times
    But I was acting in Christmas plays
While they were taken to pantomimes.
    I didn't envy their Eton suits,
Their children's dances and Christmas trees.
    My life had wonderful substitutes
For such conventional treats as these.
    I didn't envy their country larks,
Their organized games in panelled halls:
    While they made snowmen in stately parks
I was counting the curtain calls.

    I remember the auditions, the nerve-racking auditions:
    Darkened auditorium and empty, dusty stage,
    Little girls in ballet dresses practising 'positions',
    Gentlemen with pince-nez asking you your age.
    Hopefulness and nervousness struggling within you,
    Dreading that familiar phrase, 'Thank you dear, no more.'
    Straining every muscle, every tendon, every sinew
    To do your dance much better than you'd ever done before.
    Think of your performance. Never mind the others,
    Never mind the pianist, talent must prevail.
    Never mind the baleful eyes of other children's mothers
    Glaring from the corners and willing you to fail.

I can remember. I can remember.
The months of November and December
    Were more significant to me
Than other months could ever be
    For they were the months of high romance
When destiny waited on tip-toe,
    When every boy actor stood a chance
Of getting into a Christmas show,
    Not for me the dubious heaven
Of being some prefect's protégé!
    Not for me the Second Eleven.
For me, two performances a day.

Ah those first rehearsals! Only very few lines:
Rushing home to mother, learning them by heart,
'Enter Left through window' – Dots to mark the cue lines:
'Exit with the others' – Still it *was* a part.
Opening performance; legs a bit unsteady,
Dedicated tension, shivers down my spine,
Powder, grease and eye-black, sticks of make-up ready
Lcichner number three and number five and number nine.
World of strange enchantment, magic for a small boy
Dreaming of the future, reaching for the crown,
Rigid in the dressing-room, listening for the call-boy
'Overture Beginner – Everybody Down!' ➥

I can remember. I can remember.
The months of November and December,
    Although climatically cold and damp,
Meant more to me than Aladdin's lamp.
I see myself, having got a job,
Walking on wings along the Strand,
Uncertain whether to laugh or sob
And clutching tightly my mother's hand,
    I never cared who scored the goal
Or which side won the silver cup,
    I never learned to bat or bowl
But I heard the curtain going up.

Noel Coward

The Adventures of Isabel

Isabel met an enormous bear,
Isabel, Isabel, didn't care;
The bear was hungry, the bear was ravenous,
The bear's big mouth was cruel and cavernous.
The bear said, Isabel, glad to meet you,
How do, Isabel, now I'll eat you!
Isabel, Isabel, didn't worry,
Isabel didn't scream or scurry,
She washed her hands and she straightened her hair up,
Then Isabel quietly ate the bear up.

Once in a night as black as pitch
Isabel met a wicked witch.
The witch's face was cross and wrinkled,
The witch's gums with teeth were sprinkled.
Ho ho, Isabel! the old witch crowed,
I'll turn you into an ugly toad!
Isabel, Isabel, didn't worry,
Isabel didn't scream or scurry,
She showed no rage, she showed no rancor,
But she turned the witch into milk and drank her. ⇝

Isabel met a hideous giant,
Isabel continued self-reliant.
The giant was hairy, the giant was horrid,
He had one eye in the middle of his forehead.
Good morning, Isabel, the giant said,
I'll grind your bones to make my bread.
Isabel, Isabel, didn't worry,
Isabel didn't scream or scurry.
She nibbled the zwieback that she always fed off,
And when it was gone, she cut the giant's head off.

Isabel met a troublesome doctor,
He punched and he poked till he really shocked her.
The doctor's talk was of coughs and chills
And the doctor's satchel bulged with pills.
The doctor said unto Isabel,
Swallow this, it will make you well.
Isabel, Isabel, didn't worry,
Isabel didn't scream or scurry.
She took those pills from the pill concoctor,
And Isabel calmly cured the doctor.

Isabel once was asleep in bed
When a horrible dream crawled into her head.
It was worse than a dinosaur, worse than a shark,
Worse than an octopus oozing in the dark,
'Boo!' said the dream, with a dreadful grin,
'I'm going to scare you out of your skin!'
Isabel, Isabel, didn't worry,
Isabel didn't scream or scurry,
Isabel had a cleverer scheme;
She just woke up and fooled that dream.

Whenever you meet a bugaboo
Remember what Isabel used to do.
Don't scream when the bugaboo says 'Boo!'
Just look it in the eye and say, 'Boo to you!'
That's how to banish a bugaboo;
Isabel did it and so can you!
Boooooo to you.

Ogden Nash

maggie and milly and molly and may

maggie and milly and molly and may
went down to the beach(to play one day)

and maggie discovered a shell that sang
so sweetly she couldn't remember her troubles,and

milly befriended a stranded star
whose rays five languid fingers were;

and molly was chased by a horrible thing
which raced sideways while blowing bubbles:and

may came home with a smooth round stone
as small as a world and as large as alone.

For whatever we lose(like a you or a me)
it's always ourselves we find in the sea

E. E. Cummings

Equestrienne

See, they are clearing the sawdust course
For the girl in pink on the milk-white horse.
Her spangles twinkle; his pale flanks shine,
Every hair of his tail is fine
And bright as a comet's: his mane blows free,
And she points a toe and bends a knee,
And while his hoofbeats fall like rain
Over and over and over again.
And nothing that moves on land or sea
Will seem so beautiful to me
As the girl in pink on the milk-white horse
Cantering over the sawdust course.

Rachel Field

Brendon Gallacher

for my brother Maxie

He was seven and I was six, my Brendon Gallacher.
He was Irish and I was Scottish, my Brendon Gallacher.
His father was in prison; he was a cat burglar.
My father was a communist party full-time worker.
He had six brothers and I had one, my Brendon Gallacher.

He would hold my hand and take me by the river
Where we'd talk all about his family being poor.
He'd get his mum out of Glasgow when he got older.
A wee holiday some place nice. Some place far.
I'd tell my mum about my Brendon Gallacher

How his mum drank and his daddy was a cat burglar.
And she'd say, 'Why not have him round to dinner?'
No, no, I'd say, he's got big holes in his trousers.
I like meeting him by the burn in the open air.
Then one day after we'd been friends two years,

One day when it was pouring and I was indoors,
My mum says to me, 'I was talking to Mrs Moir
Who lives next door to your Brendon Gallacher
Didn't you say his address was 24 Novar?
She says there are no Gallachers at 24 Novar

There never have been any Gallachers next door.'
And he died then, my Brendon Gallacher,
Flat out on my bedroom floor, his spiky hair,
His impish grin, his funny flapping ear.
Oh Brendon. Oh my Brendon Gallacher.

Jackie Kay

If No One Ever Marries Me

If no one ever marries me, –
    And I don't see why they should,
For nurse says I'm not pretty,
    And I'm seldom very good –

If no one ever marries me
    I shan't mind very much;
I shall buy a squirrel in a cage,
    And a little rabbit-hutch:

I shall have a cottage near a wood,
    And a pony all my own,
And a little lamb, quite clean and tame,
    That I can take to town:

And when I'm getting really old, –
    At twenty-eight or nine –
I shall buy a little orphan girl
    And bring her up as mine.

Laurence Alma-Tadema

Colouring In

And staying inside the lines
Is fine, but ...
I like it when stuff leaks –
When the blue bird and the blue sky
Are just one blur of blue blue flying,
And the feeling of the feathers in the air
And the wind along the blade of wing
Is a long gash of smudgy colour.
I like it when the flowers and the sunshine
Puddle red and yellow into orange,
The way the hot sun on my back
Lulls me – muddles me – sleepy
In the scented garden,
Makes me part of the picture ...
Part of the place.

Jan Dean

Amanda!

Don't bite your nails, Amanda!
Don't hunch your shoulders, Amanda!
Stop that slouching and sit up straight,
Amanda!

(There is a languid, emerald sea,
where the sole inhabitant is me –
a mermaid, drifting blissfully.)

Did you finish your homework, Amanda?
Did you tidy your room, Amanda?
I thought I told you to clean your shoes,
Amanda!

(I am an orphan, roaming the street.
I pattern soft dust with my hushed, bare feet.
The silence is golden, the freedom is sweet.)

Don't eat that chocolate, Amanda!
Remember your acne, Amanda!
Will you please look at me when I'm speaking to you,
Amanda!

(I am Rapunzel, I have not a care;
life in a tower is tranquil and rare;
I'll certainly *never* let down my bright hair!)

Stop that sulking at once, Amanda!
You're always so moody, Amanda!
Anyone would think that I nagged at you,
Amanda!

Robin Klein

Halo

I was as good as gold, an angel, said ta very much, no thanks,
yes *please*, smiled politely
when I said hello, helped out, tried;
so it came to pass I awoke
and there in the bed
next to my head on the pillow
a halo glowed, a hoop-la of gold.
I didn't faint or scream
or wake up and find it was only a dream,
but went to the mirror
and stared at the icon of me –
acne, bad hair, pyjamas, sticky-out ears, halo.

On the way to school
I swished the halo along with a stick
up the road, down the hill, round the bend
where I frisbeed it to my good friend Dominic Gill,
who caught it, said *What's this then, mate?*
A halo, chum, I'm a saint.
No, you ain't.
Delicate, quaint, the halo settled itself
at the back of my head,
shining and bright,
shedding its numinous light all through Maths,
double English, RK, PE, lunch, History, silent reading.
The teachers stared
but left me alone,
and I kept my eyes on the numbers, the verbs,
the prophets, the dates, the poem,
till the bell rang, then legged it for home.

But some big kids snatched my halo
as I ran through the park;
tossed it between them, kicked it, flicked it,
lobbed it,
far too high for me,
into the outstretched branches of a tree.
Then dusk lapped at my feet
and the navy-blue sea of the sky
floated the moon
as I watched the light of my halo dissolve
to the pinprick glow of a worm,
and heard the loudening shout of a voice
calling, calling my human name.

Carol Ann Duffy

Good Girls

Good girls
will always go like clockwork
home from school,

through the iron gates
where clambering boys
whisper and pull,

past houses
where curtains twitch
and a fingery witch beckons,

by the graveyard
where stone angels stir,
itching their wings,

past tunnelled woods
where forgotten wolves wait
for prey,

past dens
and caves and darknesses
they go like clockwork;

and when they come
to school again
their homework's done.

Irene Rawnsley

WOMEN

Minnie and Winnie

Minnie and Winnie
    Slept in a shell.
Sleep, little ladies!
    And they slept well.

Pink was the shell within,
    Silver without;
Sounds of the great sea
    Wandered about.

Sleep, little ladies,
    Wake not soon!
Echo on echo
    Dies to the moon.

Two bright stars
    Peeped into the shell.
'What are they dreaming of?
    Who can tell?'

Started a green linnet
    Out of the croft;
Wake, little ladies,
    The sun is aloft!

Alfred, Lord Tennyson

Tarantella

Do you remember an Inn,
Miranda?
Do you remember an Inn?
And the tedding and the spreading
Of the straw for a bedding,
And the fleas that tease in the High Pyrenees,
And the wine that tasted of the tar?
And the cheers and the jeers of the young muleteers
(Under the vine of the dark verandah)?
Do you remember an Inn, Miranda,
Do you remember an Inn?
And the cheers and the jeers of the young muleteers
Who hadn't got a penny,
And who weren't paying any,
And the hammer at the doors and the Din?
And the Hip! Hop! Hap!
Of the clap
Of the hands to the twirl and the swirl
Of the girl gone chancing,
Glancing,
Dancing,
Backing and advancing,
Snapping of a clapper to the spin
Out and in –
And the Ting, Tong, Tang of the Guitar!

Do you remember an Inn,
Miranda?
Do you remember an Inn!
Never more;
Miranda,
Never more.
Only the high peaks hoar:
And Aragon a torrent at the door.
No sound
In the walls of the Halls where falls
The tread
Of the feet of the dead to the ground
No sound:
But the boom
Of the far Waterfall like Doom.

Hilaire Belloc

Unwilling Country Life

She went, to plain-work, and to purling brooks,
Old fashioned halls, dull Aunts, and croaking rooks:
She went from Opera, Park, Assembly, Play,
To morning walks, and prayers three hours a day;
To part her time 'twixt reading and bohea;
To muse, and spill her solitary tea
Or o'er cold coffee trifle with the spoon,
Count the slow clock, and dine exact at noon;
Divert her eyes with pictures in the fire,
Hum half a tune, tell stories to the squire;
Up to her godly garret after seven,
There starve and pray, for that's the way to heaven.
Some Squire, perhaps you take delight to rack;
Whose game is Whist, whose treat, a toast in sack;
Who visits with a gun, presents you birds,
Then gives a smacking buss, and cries – 'No words!'
Or with his hounds comes hollowing from the stable,
Makes love with nods, and knees beneath a table;
Whose laughs are hearty, though his jests are coarse,
And loves you best of all things – but his horse.

Alexander Pope

Annabel-Emily

Annabel-Emily Huntington-Horne
Who lives at Threepenny Cam
From the very first moment that she was born
Would eat nothing whatever but jam.

They offered her milk, they offered her bread,
They offered her biscuits and beans
But Annabel-Emily shook her head
And made the most horrible scenes.

They offered her chicken, and also a choice
Of sausage or cheese or Spam
But Annabel screamed at the top of her voice,
'Can't you see what I'm wanting is JAM?'

Her parents they wept like the watery bay
And they uttered and spluttered such cries
As, 'She's perfectly certain to waste away
In front of our very own eyes!'

But Annabel-Emily Huntington-Horne,
Her hair the colour of snow,
Still lives in the cottage where she was born
A hundred years ago.

Her tooth is as sugary sweet today
As ever it was before
And as for her hundred years, they say
She's good for a hundred more.

She's pots of apricot, strawberry, peach
In twos and threes and fours
On yards and yards of shelves that reach
From the ceilings to the floors.

She's jars of currants red and black
On every chest and chair
And plum and gooseberry in a stack
On every step of the stair.

Raspberry, cranberry, blackberry, or
Apple, damson, quince –
There never was better jam before
Nor will ever be better since.

For Annabel of Threepenny Cam,
Whose ways are quite well known,
Has never been one for boughten jam
And always makes her own.

But if, when you are passing by,
She invites you for tea and a treat
Be careful just how you reply
If your taste and tooth aren't sweet:

Or it's certain (all the neighbours warn)
You'll be in a terrible jam
With Annabel-Emily Huntington-Horne
Who lives at Threepenny Cam.

Charles Causley

The Ice

Her day out from the workhouse-ward, she stands,
A grey-haired woman decent and precise,
With prim black bonnet and neat paisley shawl,
Among the other children by the stall,
And with grave relish eats a penny ice.

To wizened toothless gums with quaking hands
She holds it, shuddering with delicious cold,
Nor heeds the jeering laughter of young men—
The happiest, in her innocence, of all:
For, while their insolent youth must soon grow old,
She, who's been old, is now a child again.

Wilfrid Gibson

166

The History of Sixteen Wonderful Old Women

MISTRESS TOWL
There was an Old Woman named Towl,
Who went out to Sea with her Owl,
    But the Owl was Sea-sick,
    And scream'd for Physic;
Which sadly annoy'd Mistress Towl.

OLD WOMAN OF FRANCE
There came an Old Woman from France,
Who taught grown-up Children to dance,
    But they were so stiff,
    She sent them home in a miff;
This sprightly Old Woman from France.

OLD WOMAN OF BATH
There was an Old Woman of Bath,
And She was as thin as a Lath,
    She was brown as a berry,
    with a Nose like a Cherry;
This skinny Old Woman of Bath.

OLD WOMAN OF CROYDON
There was an Old Woman of Croydon,
To look young she affected the Hoyden,
    And would jump and would skip,
    Till she put out her hip;
Alas poor Old Woman of Croydon.

OLD WOMAN OF HARROW

There was an Old Woman of Harrow,
Who visited in a Wheel barrow,
    And her servant before,
    Knock'd loud at each door;
To announce the Old Woman of Harrow.

OLD WOMAN OF GLOSTER

There was an Old Woman at Gloster,
Whose Parrot two Guineas it cost her.
    But his tongue never ceasing,
    Was vastly displeasing;
To the talkative Woman of Gloster.

OLD WOMAN OF EXETER

There dwelt an Old Woman at Exeter,
When visitors came it sore vexed her.
    So for fear they should eat,
    She lock'd up all the meat;
This stingy Old Woman of Exeter.

OLD WOMAN OF GOSPORT

Then was an Old Woman of Gosport,
And she was one of the cross sort.
    When she dress'd for the Ball,
    Her wig was too small;
Which enrag'd this Old Lady of Gosport.

OLD WOMAN OF LYNN

There liv'd an Old Woman at Lynn
Whose Nose very near touch'd her chin.
  You may easy suppose,
  She had plenty of Beaux;
This charming Old Woman of Lynn.

OLD WOMAN OF LEITH

There was an Old Woman of Leith,
Who had a sad pain in her Teeth.
  But the Blacksmith uncouth.
  Scar'd the pain from her tooth;
Which rejoic'd the Old Woman of Leith.

OLD WOMAN OF SURREY

There was an Old Woman in Surrey,
Who was morn noon and night in a hurry,
  Call'd her Husband a Fool,
  Drove her Children to School;
The worrying Old Woman of Surrey.

OLD WOMAN OF DEVON

There was an Old Woman of Devon,
Who rose every morning at seven,
  For her house to provide,
  And to warm her inside;
This provident Woman of Devon.

OLD WOMAN OF SPAIN

There was an Old Woman in Spain,
To be civil went much 'gainst her grain,
    Yet she danc'd a fandango,
    With General Fernando;
This whimsical Woman of Spain.

OLD WOMAN OF NORWICH

There was an Old Woman at Norwich,
Who liv'd upon nothing but Porridge,
    Parading the Town,
    Made a cloak of her Gown;
This thrifty Old Woman of Norwich.

OLD WOMAN OF EALING

There was an Old Woman of Ealing,
She jumped till her head touch'd the Ceiling
    When 2 1 6 4.
    Was announc'd at her Door;
As a prize to th' Old Woman of Ealing.

OLD WOMAN OF LEEDS

There was an Old Woman at Leeds,
Who spent all her time in good deeds,
    She work'd for the Poor,
    Till her fingers were sore;
This pious Old Woman of Leeds.

Anon.

LOVE

The Janitor's Boy

Oh I'm in love with the janitor's boy,
 And the janitor's boy loves me;
He's going to hunt for a desert isle
 In our geography.

A desert isle with spicy trees
 Somewhere near Sheepshead Bay;
A right nice place, just fit for two
 Where we can live alway.

Oh I'm in love with the janitor's boy,
 He's busy as he can be;
And down in the cellar he's making a raft
 Out of an old scttee.

He'll carry me off, I know that he will,
 For his hair is exceedingly red;
And the only thing that occurs to me
 Is to dutifully shiver in bed.

The day that we sail, I shall leave this brief note,
 For my parents I hate to annoy:
'I have flown away to an isle in the bay
 With the janitor's red-haired boy.'

Nathalia Crane

Romance

I will make you brooches and toys for your delight
Of bird-song at morning and star-shine at night.
I will make a palace fit for you and me,
Of green days in forests and blue days at sea.

I will make my kitchen, and you shall keep your room,
Where white flows the river and bright blows the broom,
And you shall wash your linen and keep your body white
In rainfall at morning and dewfall at night.

And this shall be for music when no one else is near,
The fine song for singing, the rare song to hear!
That only I remember, that only you admire,
Of the broad road that stretches and the roadside fire.

Robert Louis Stevenson

Expecting Visitors

I heard you were coming and
Thrum thrum thrum
Went something in my heart like a
Drum drum drum.

I briskly walked down the
Street street street
To buy lovely food for us to
Eat eat eat.

I cleaned the house and filled it with
Flowers flowers flowers
And asked the sun to drink up the
Showers showers showers.

Steadily purring
Thrum, thrum, thrum
Went the drum in my heart because
You'd come, come, come.

Jenny Joseph

174

Love Hearts
sweets for the sweet

February 14th
playing Cupid
girl on my table acting stupid
passing sweets to me.

They say  I Love You

an You're so Fine,

my friends crease up at Please Be Mine.

She must have packets of them.

All through maths they come

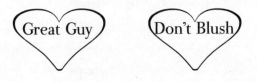 Great Guy   Don't Blush

Then Trust Me – that kind of mush

It's really getting to me.

Then 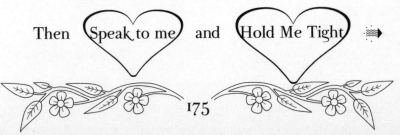 Speak to me and Hold Me Tight ➤

175

So at break I go up to her. All right!
She blinks at me. Her smile is growing.

Offers a sweet – ❤️ Be Kind is showing.

I snatch them, push her, run off crowing.

All afternoon I'm thinking how she felt.
I smell the sweet and sickly scent
as pastel messages fizz and melt.

I send back ❤️ Crazy! And ❤️ No Chance.

I nudge and snigger ❤️ Wanna Dance?

I chuck ❤️ No Way and flick ❤️ Big Deal

I throw ❤️ In Love and make her squeal

Then,

when all my friends have gone away

I quietly give her ❤️ Don't Cry

and ❤️ U.R.O.K.

Michaela Morgan

The Twelve Days of Christmas

On the first day of Christmas
my true love sent to me:
    A partridge in a pear tree

On the second day of Christmas
my true love sent to me:
    Two turtle doves
    and a partridge in a pear tree

On the third day of Christmas
my true love sent to me:
    Three French hens
    Two turtle doves
    and a partridge in a pear tree

On the fourth day of Christmas
my true love sent to me:
    Four calling birds
    Three French hens
    Two turtle doves
    and a partridge in a pear tree

On the fifth day of Christmas
my true love sent to me:
    Five gold rings
    Four calling birds
    Three French hens
    Two turtle doves
    and a partridge in a pear tree

On the sixth day of Christmas
my true love sent to me:
    Six geese a-laying
    Five gold rings
    Four calling birds
    Three French hens
    Two turtle doves
    and a partridge in a pear tree

On the seventh day of Christmas
my true love sent to me:
    Seven swans a-swimming
    Six geese a-laying
    Five gold rings
    Four calling birds
    Three French hens
    Two turtle doves
    and a partridge in a pear tree

On the eighth day of Christmas,
my true love sent to me:
    Eight maids a-milking
    Seven swans a-swimming
    Six geese a-laying
    Five gold rings
    Four calling birds
    Three French hens
    Two turtle doves
    And a partridge in a pear tree

On the ninth day of Christmas,
my true love sent to me:
    Nine ladies dancing
    Eight maids a-milking
    Seven swans a-swimming
    Six geese a-laying
    Five gold rings
    Four calling birds
    Three French hens
    Two turtle doves
    And a partridge in a pear tree

On the tenth day of Christmas,
my true love sent to me:
    Ten lords a-leaping
    Nine ladies dancing
    Eight maids a-milking
    Seven swans a-swimming
    Six geese a-laying
    Five gold rings
    Four calling birds
    Three French hens
    Two turtle doves
    And a partridge in a pear tree

On the eleventh day of Christmas,
my true love sent to me:
    Eleven pipers piping
    Ten lords a-leaping
    Nine ladies dancing
    Eight maids a-milking
    Seven swans a-swimming
    Six geese a-laying
    Five gold rings
    Four calling birds
    Three French hens
    Two turtle doves
    And a partridge in a pear tree

On the twelfth day of Christmas
my true love sent to me:
    Twelve drummers drumming
    Eleven pipers piping
    Ten lords a-leaping
    Nine ladies dancing
    Eight maids a-milking
    Seven swans a-swimming
    Six geese a-laying
    Five gold rings
    Four calling birds
    Three French hens
    Two turtle doves
    and a partridge in a pear tree

Anon.

Dear True Love

Leaping and dancing
Means to-ing and fro-ing;
Drummers and pipers –
Loud banging and blowing;
Even a pear tree
Needs room to grow in.

Goose eggs and gold top
When I'm trying to slim?
And seven swans swimming?
Where could they swim?

Mine is a small house,
Your gifts are grand;
One ring at a time
Is enough for this hand.

Hens, colly birds, doves –
A gastronome's treat.
But love, I did tell you,
I've given up meat.

Your fairy-tale presents
Are wasted on me.
Just send me your love
And set all the birds free.

U. A. Fanthorpe

Party

Sitting on the stairs,
you tell me that when you were five
a boy called David Bird tried to kiss you,
missed, and fell into a bed of nettles.

I want to kiss you now,
but what would I fall off,
and what would I fall into?

Too late I move, indecisively,
and fall into the nettles.

Someone takes you gently by the hand,
smoothes your hair,
leads you back into the party.

Adrian Henri

Indoor Games near Newbury

In among the silver birches,
Winding ways of tarmac wander
And the signs to Bussock Bottom,
Tussock Wood and Windy Brake,
Gabled lodges, tile-hung churches
Catch the lights of our Lagonda
As we drive to Wendy's party,
Lemon curd and Christmas cake

Rich the makes of motor whirring,
Past the pine plantation purring
Come up Hupmobile Delage.
Short the way our chauffeurs travel,
Crunching over private gravel,
Each from out his warm garáge.

O but Wendy, when the carpet
Yielded to my indoor pumps.
There you stood, your gold hair streaming,
Handsome in the hall light gleaming
There you looked and there you led me
Off into the game of Clumps ⇒

Then the new Victrola playing;
And your funny uncle saying
'Choose your partners for a foxtrot!
Dance until it's tea o'clock!
Come on, young 'uns, foot it feetly!'
Was it chance that paired us neatly?
I, who loved you so completely.
You, who pressed me closely to you,
Hard against your party frock.

'Meet me when you've finished eating!'
So we met and no one found us.
O that dark and furry cupboard,
While the rest played hide-and-seek.
Holding hands our two hearts beating.
In the bedroom silence round us
Holding hands and hardly hearing
Sudden footstep, thud and shriek.

Love that lay too deep for kissing.
'Where is Wendy? Wendy's missing!'
Love so pure it had to end.
Love so strong that I was frighten'd
When you gripped my fingers tight.
And hugging, whispered 'I'm your friend.'

Goodbye Wendy. Send the fairies,
Pinewood elf and larch tree gnome.
Spingle-spangled stars are peeping
At the lush Lagonda creeping
Down the winding ways of tarmac
To the leaded lights of home.

There among the silver birches,
All the bells of all the churches
Sounded in the bath-waste running
Out into the frosty air.
Wendy speeded my undressing.
Wendy is the sheet's caressing
Wendy bending gives a blessing.
Holds me as I drift to dreamland
Safe inside my slumber-wear.

John Betjeman

A Birthday

My heart is like a singing bird
    Whose nest is in a watered shoot;
My heart is like an apple-tree
    Whose boughs are bent with thick-set fruit;
My heart is like a rainbow shell
    That paddles in a halcyon sea;
My heart is gladder than all these
    Because my love is come to me.

Raise me a dais of silk and down;
    Hang it with vair and purple dyes;
Carve it in doves, and pomegranates,
    And peacocks with a hundred eyes;
Work it in gold and silver grapes,
    In leaves, and silver fleurs-de-lys;
Because the birthday of my life
    Is come, my love is come to me.

Christina Rossetti

from The Princess

Now sleeps the crimson petal, now the white;
Nor waves the cypress in the palace walk;
Nor winks the gold fin in the porphyry font:
The fire-fly wakens: waken thou with me.

Now droops the milkwhite peacock like a ghost,
And like a ghost she glimmers on to me.

Now lies the Earth all Danae to the stars,
And all thy heart lies open unto me.

Now slides the silent meteor on, and leaves
A shining furrow, as thy thoughts in me.

Now folds the lily all her sweetness up,
And slips into the bosom of the lake:
So fold thyself, my dearest, thou, and slip
Into my bosom and be lost in me.

Alfred, Lord Tennyson

The Passionate Shepherd to His Love

Come live with me and be my Love,
And we will all the pleasures prove
That valleys, groves, hills, and fields,
Woods, or steepy mountains yields.

And we will sit upon the rocks
Seeing the shepherds feed their flocks,
By shallow rivers, to whose falls
Melodious birds sing madrigals.

And I will make thee beds of roses
And a thousand fragrant posies,
A cap of flowers, and a kirtle
Embroidered all with leaves of myrtle;

A gown made of the finest wool,
Which from our pretty lambs we pull;
Fair linèd slippers for the cold,
With buckles of the purest gold;

A belt of straw and ivy buds
With coral clasps and amber studs;
And if these pleasures may thee move,
Come live with me and be my Love.

The shepherd swains shall dance and sing
For thy delight each May morning:
If these delights thy mind may move,
Then live with me and be my Love.

Christopher Marlowe

Love You More

Do I love you
to the moon and back?
No I love you
more than that

I love you to the desert sands
the mountains, stars
the planets and

I love you to the deepest sea
and deeper still
through history

Before beyond I love you then
I love you now
I'll love you when

The sun's gone out
the moon's gone home
and all the stars are fully grown

When I no longer say these words
I'll give them to the winds, the birds
so that they will still be heard

I love you

James Carter

How Do I Love Thee?

How do I love thee? Let me count the ways.
I love thee to the depth and breadth and height
My soul can reach, when feeling out of sight
For the ends of Being and ideal Grace.
I love thee to the level of every day's
Most quiet need, by sun and candle-light.
I love thee freely, as men strive for right;
I love thee purely, as they turn from praise.
I love thee with the passion put to use
In my old griefs, and with my childhood's faith.
I love thee with a love I seemed to lose
With my lost saints – I love thee with the breath,
Smiles, tears, of all my life! – and, if God choose,
I shall but love thee better after death.

Elizabeth Barrett Browning

Sally in our Alley

Of all the girls that are so smart
    There's none like pretty Sally;
She is the darling of my heart,
    And she lives in our alley.
There is no lady in the land
    Is half so sweet as Sally;
She is the darling of my heart,
    And she lives in our alley.

Her father he makes cabbage-nets,
    And through the streets does cry 'em;
Her mother she sells laces long
    To such as please to buy 'em.
But sure such folks could ne'er beget
    So sweet a girl as Sally!
She is the darling of my heart,
    And she lives in our alley.

When she is by, I leave my work,
    I love her so sincerely;
My master comes like any Turk,
    And bangs me most severely.
But let him bang his bellyful,
    I'll bear it all for Sally;
She is the darling of my heart,
    And she lives in our alley.

Of all the days that's in the week
     I dearly love but one day,
And that's the day that comes betwixt
     A Saturday and Monday;
For then I'm drest all in my best
     To walk abroad with Sally;
She is the darling of my heart,
     And she lives in our alley.

My master carries me to church,
     And often am I blamèd
Because I leave him in the lurch
     As soon as text is namèd.
I leave the church in sermon-time
     And slink away to Sally;
She is the darling of my heart,
     And she lives in our alley.

When Christmas comes about again,
     O, then I shall have money;
I'll hoard it up, and box it all,
     I'll give it to my honey.
I would it were ten thousand pound,
     I'd give it all to Sally;
She is the darling of my heart,
     And she lives in our alley.

My master and the neighbours all
    Make game of me and Sally,
And, but for her, I'd better be
    A slave and row a galley;
But when my seven long years are out,
    O, then I'll marry Sally;
O, then we'll wed, and then we'll bed,
    But not in our alley.

Henry Carey

Renouncement

I must not think of thee; and, tired yet strong,
I shun the thought that lurks in all delight –
The thought of thee – and in the blue Heaven's height,
And in the sweetest passage of a song.
O just beyond the fairest thoughts that throng
This breast, the thought of thee waits hidden yet bright;
But it must never, never come in sight;
I must stop short of thee the whole day long.

But when sleep comes to close each difficult day,
When night gives pause to the long watch I keep,
And all my bonds I needs must loose apart,
Must doff my will as raiment laid away,
With the first dream that comes with the first sleep
I run, I run, I am gathered to thy heart.

Alice Meynell

A Quoi Bon Dire

Seventeen years ago you said
    Something that sounded like Good-bye:
    And everybody thinks you are dead
        But I.

    So I as I grow stiff and cold
To this and that say Good-bye too;
    And everybody sees that I am old
        But you.

    And one fine morning in a sunny lane
Some boy and girl will meet and kiss and swear
    That nobody can love their way again
        While over there
You will have smiled, I shall have tossed your hair.

Charlotte Mew

As I Walked Out One Evening

As I walked out one evening,
    Walking down Bristol Street,
The crowds upon the pavement
    Were fields of harvest wheat.

And down by the brimming river
    I heard a lover sing
Under an arch of the railway:
    'Love has no ending.

'I'll love you, dear, I'll love you
    Till China and Africa meet,
And the river jumps over the mountain
    And the salmon sing in the street,

'I'll love you till the ocean
    Is folded and hung up to dry
And the seven stars go squawking
    Like geese about the sky.

'The years shall run like rabbits,
    For in my arms I hold
The Flower of the Ages,
    And the first love of the world.'

But all the clocks in the city
    Began to whirr and chime:
'O let not Time deceive you,
    You cannot conquer Time.

'In the burrows of the Nightmare
        Where Justice naked is,
Time watches from the shadow
        And coughs when you would kiss.

'In headaches and in worry
        Vaguely life leaks away,
And Time will have his fancy
        Tomorrow or today.

'Into many a green valley
        Drifts the appalling snow;
Time breaks the threaded dances
        And the diver's brilliant bow.

'O plunge your hands in water,
        Plunge them in up to the wrist;
Stare, stare in the basin
        And wonder what you've missed.

'The glacier knocks in the cupboard,
        The desert sighs in the bed,
And the crack in the teacup opens
        A lane to the land of the dead.

'Where the beggars raffle the banknotes
        And the Giant is enchanting to Jack,
And the Lily-white Boy is a Roarer,
        And Jill goes down on her back. ⇒

'O look, look in the mirror,
        O look in your distress;
Life remains a blessing
        Although you cannot bless.

'O stand, stand at the window
        As the tears scald and start;
You shall love your crooked neighbour
        With your crooked heart.'

It was late, late in the evening,
        The lovers they were gone;
The clocks had ceased their chiming,
        And the deep river ran on.

W. H. Auden

Sonnet 18

Shall I compare thee to a summer's day?
Thou art more lovely and more temperate:
Rough winds do shake the darling buds of May,
And summer's lease hath all too short a date:
Sometime too hot the eye of heaven shines,
And often is his gold complexion dimm'd;
And every fair from fair sometime declines,
By chance or nature's changing course untrimm'd;
But thy eternal summer shall not fade,
Nor lose possession of that fair thou ow'st;
Nor shall Death brag thou wander'st in his shade,
When in eternal lines to time thou grow'st:
     So long as men can breathe, or eyes can see,
     So long lives this, and this gives life to thee.

William Shakespeare

STORIES

La Belle Dame Sans Merci

'O what can ail thee, Knight-at-arms,
Alone and palely loitering?
The sedge is wither'd from the lake,
And no birds sing.

'O what can ail thee, Knight-at-arms,
So haggard and so woebegone?
The squirrel's granary is full,
And the harvest's done.

'I see a lily on thy brow
With anguish moist and fever dew,
And on thy cheek a fading rose
Fast withereth too.'

'I met a lady in the meads
Full beautiful – a faery's child,
Her hair was long, her foot was light,
And her eyes were wild.

'I made a garland for her head,
And bracelets too, and fragrant zone;
She look'd at me as she did love,
And made sweet moan.

'I set her on my pacing steed,
And nothing else saw all day long,
For sidelong would she bend and sing
A faery's song.

'She found me roots of relish sweet,
And honey wild and manna dew,
And sure in language strange she said,
"I love thee true."

'She took me to her elfin grot,
And there she wept and sigh'd full sore;
And there I shut her wild wild eyes
With kisses four.

'And there she lulled me asleep,
And there I dream'd – Ah! woe betide!
The latest dream I ever dream'd
On the cold hill's side.

'I saw pale kings and princes too,
Pale warriors, death-pale were they all;
Who cried – "La Belle Dame sans Merci
Hath thee in thrall!"

'I saw their starv'd lips in the gloam
With horrid warning gaped wide,
And I awoke and found me here
On the cold hill's side.

'And this is why I sojourn here
Alone and palely loitering,
Though the sedge is wither'd from the lake,
And no birds sing.'

John Keats

The Song of Wandering Aengus

I went out to the hazel wood,
Because a fire was in my head,
And cut and peeled a hazel wand,
And hooked a berry to a thread,
And when white moths were on the wing,
And moth-like stars were flickering out,
I dropped the berry in a stream
And caught a little silver trout.

When I had laid it on the floor
I went to blow the fire a-flame,
But something rustled on the floor,
And someone called me by my name:
It had become a glimmering girl
With apple blossoms in her hair
Who called me by my name and ran
And faded through the brightening air.

Though I am old with wandering
Through hollow lands and hilly lands,
I will find out where she has gone,
And kiss her lips and take her hands;
And walk among long dappled grass,
And pluck till time and times are done,
The silver apples of the moon,
The golden apples of the sun.

W. B. Yeats

The Jumblies

They went to sea in a Sieve, they did,
    In a Sieve they went to sea:
In spite of all their friends could say,
On a winter's morn, on a stormy day,
    In a Sieve they went to sea!
And when the Sieve turned round and round,
And every one cried, 'You'll all be drowned!'
They called aloud, 'Our Sieve ain't big,
But we don't care a button! we don't care a fig!
    In a Sieve we'll go to sea!'
      Far and few, far and few,
        Are the lands where the Jumblies live;
      Their heads are green, and their hands are blue,
        And they went to sea in a Sieve.

They sailed away in a Sieve, they did,
    In a Sieve they sailed so fast,
With only a beautiful pea-green veil
Tied with a riband by way of a sail,
    To a small tobacco-pipe mast;
And every one said, who saw them go,
'O won't they be soon upset, you know!
For the sky is dark, and the voyage is long,
And happen what may, it's extremely wrong
    In a Sieve to sail so fast!'
      Far and few, far and few,
        Are the lands where the Jumblies live;
      Their heads are green, and their hands are blue,
        And they went to sea in a Sieve.

The water it soon came in, it did,
    The water it soon came in;
So to keep them dry, they wrapped their feet
In a pinky paper all folded neat,
    And they fastened it down with a pin.
And they passed the night in a crockery-jar,
And each of them said, 'How wise we are!
Though the sky be dark, and the voyage be long,
Yet we never can think we were rash or wrong,
    While round in our Sieve we spin!'
        Far and few, far and few,
            Are the lands where the Jumblies live;
        Their heads are green, and their hands are blue,
            And they went to sea in a Sieve.

And all night long they sailed away;
    And when the sun went down,
They whistled and warbled a moony song
To the echoing sound of a coppery gong,
    In the shade of the mountains brown.
O Timballo! How happy we are,
When we live in a Sieve and a crockery-jar,
And all night long in the moonlight pale,
We sail away with a pea-green sail,
    In the shade of the mountains brown!'
        Far and few, far and few,
            Are the lands where the Jumblies live;
        Their heads are green, and their hands are blue,
            And they went to sea in a Sieve.

They sailed to the Western Sea, they did,
  To a land all covered with trees,
And they bought an Owl, and a useful Cart,
And a pound of Rice, and a Cranberry Tart,
  And a hive of silvery Bees.
And they bought a Pig, and some green Jack-daws,
And a lovely Monkey with lollipop paws,
And forty bottles of Ring-Bo-Ree,
  And no end of Stilton Cheese.
    Far and few, far and few,
      Are the lands where the Jumblies live;
      Their heads are green, and their hands are blue,
      And they went to sea in a Sieve.

And in twenty years they all came back,
  In twenty years or more,
And every one said, 'How tall they've grown!
For they've been to the Lakes, and the Torrible Zone
  And the hills of the Chankly Bore;'
And they drank their health, and gave them a feast
Of dumplings made of beautiful yeast;
And every one said, 'If we only live,
We too will go to sea in a Sieve, –
  To the hills of the Chankly Bore!'
    Far and few, far and few,
      Are the lands where the Jumblies live;
      Their heads are green, and their hands are blue,
      And they went to sea in a Sieve.

                              Edward Lear

On St Catherine's Day

We are the Workhouse children,
Maids dressed in white,
Our gowns are trimmed with ribbon,
With flowers our hair is bright.

Before us walks the Master
With sure and steady tread,
And here is the tallest maid of all
A gilt crown on her head.

She bears in her hand a sceptre
Of yellow wood and tin,
And in the other a distaff
With which we may spin.

Pray give to us your ha'pennies
And give your farthings too,
That we may buy the wheels and reels
Our finest work to do.

On this day good St Catherine
To the sharp wheel has been,
Catherine, Saint of Spinners,
Catherine our Queen.

Today we shall eat rump steak
And we shall dance and game,
But the day is short and the year is long
Before it comes again.

We stand in church for the Parson,
We sit both straight and tall
As do the little stone children
That are beside the wall.

Our faces are white as paper,
Our hands are made of bone,
We may not speak the truth with our tongues
But with our eyes alone.

Though the Workhouse wall is broken,
With truest eye and clear
Watch for the Workhouse children,
For we are always here.

Charles Causley

The Lady of Shalott

Part I

On either side the river lie
Long fields of barley and of rye,
That clothe the wold and meet the sky;
And thro' the field the road runs by
To many-tower'd Camelot;
And up and down the people go,
Gazing where the lilies blow
Round an island there below,
The island of Shalott.

Willows whiten, aspens quiver,
Little breezes dusk and shiver
Thro' the wave that runs for ever
By the island in the river
Flowing down to Camelot.
Four gray walls, and four gray towers,
Overlook a space of flowers,
And the silent isle imbowers
The Lady of Shalott.

By the margin, willow veil'd,
Slide the heavy barges trail'd
By slow horses; and unhail'd
The shallop flitteth silken-sail'd
Skimming down to Camelot:
But who hath seen her wave her hand?
Or at the casement seen her stand?
Or is she known in all the land,
The Lady of Shalott?

Only reapers, reaping early
In among the bearded barley,
Hear a song that echoes cheerly
From the river winding clearly,
Down to tower'd Camelot:
And by the moon the reaper weary,
Piling sheaves in uplands airy,
Listening, whispers "'Tis the fairy
Lady of Shalott.'

Part II

There she weaves by night and day
A magic web with colours gay.
She has heard a whisper say,
A curse is on her if she stay
To look down to Camelot.
She knows not what the curse may be,
And so she weaveth steadily,
And little other care hath she,
The Lady of Shalott. ⇛

And moving thro' a mirror clear
That hangs before her all the year,
Shadows of the world appear.
There she sees the highway near
Winding down to Camelot:
There the river eddy whirls,
And there the surly village-churls,
And the red cloaks of market girls,
Pass onward from Shalott.

Sometimes a troop of damsels glad,
An abbot on an ambling pad,
Sometimes a curly shepherd-lad,
Or long-hair'd page in crimson clad,
Goes by to tower'd Camelot;
And sometimes thro' the mirror blue
The knights come riding two and two:
She hath no loyal knight and true,
The Lady of Shalott.

But in her web she still delights
To weave the mirror's magic sights,
For often thro' the silent nights
A funeral, with plumes and lights
And music, went to Camelot:
Or when the moon was overhead,
Came two young lovers lately wed:
'I am half sick of shadows,' said
The Lady of Shalott.

Part III

A bow-shot from her bower-eaves,
He rode between the barley-sheaves,
The sun came dazzling thro' the leaves,
And flamed upon the brazen greaves
    Of bold Sir Lancelot.
A red-cross knight for ever kneel'd
    To a lady in his shield,
That sparkled on the yellow field,
    Beside remote Shalott.

The gemmy bridle glitter'd free,
Like to some branch of stars we see
    Hung in the golden Galaxy.
The bridle bells rang merrily
    As he rode down to Camelot:
And from his blazon'd baldric slung
    A mighty silver bugle hung,
And as he rode his armour rung,
    Beside remote Shalott.

All in the blue unclouded weather
Thick-jewell'd shone the saddle-leather,
The helmet and the helmet-feather
Burn'd like one burning flame together,
    As he rode down to Camelot.
As often thro' the purple night,
    Below the starry clusters bright,
Some bearded meteor, trailing light,
    Moves over still Shalott. ⇝

His broad clear brow in sunlight glow'd;
On burnish'd hooves his war-horse trode;
From underneath his helmet flow'd
His coal-black curls as on he rode,
As he rode down to Camelot.
From the bank and from the river
He flash'd into the crystal mirror,
'Tirra lirra,' by the river
Sang Sir Lancelot.

She left the web, she left the loom,
She made three paces thro' the room,
She saw the water-lily bloom,
She saw the helmet and the plume,
She look'd down to Camelot.
Out flew the web and floated wide;
The mirror crack'd from side to side;
'The curse is come upon me,' cried
The Lady of Shalott.

Part IV

In the stormy east-wind straining,
The pale yellow woods were waning,
The broad stream in his banks complaining,
Heavily the low sky raining
Over tower'd Camelot;
Down she came and found a boat
Beneath a willow left afloat,
And round about the prow she wrote
The Lady of Shalott.

And down the river's dim expanse
Like some bold seer in a trance,
Seeing all his own mischance –
With a glassy countenance
Did she look to Camelot.
And at the closing of the day
She loosed the chain, and down she lay;
The broad stream bore her far away,
The Lady of Shalott.

Lying, robed in snowy white
That loosely flew to left and right –
The leaves upon her falling light –
Thro' the noises of the night
She floated down to Camelot:
And as the boat-head wound along
The willowy hills and fields among,
They heard her singing her last song,
The Lady of Shalott.

Heard a carol, mournful, holy,
Chanted loudly, chanted lowly,
Till her blood was frozen slowly,
And her eyes were darken'd wholly,
Turn'd to tower'd Camelot.
For ere she reach'd upon the tide
The first house by the water-side,
Singing in her song she died,
The Lady of Shalott.

Under tower and balcony,
By garden-wall and gallery,
A gleaming shape she floated by,
Dead-pale between the houses high,
Silent into Camelot.
Out upon the wharfs they came,
Knight and burgher, lord and dame,
And round the prow they read her name,
The Lady of Shalott.

Who is this? and what is here?
And in the lighted palace near
Died the sound of royal cheer;
And they cross'd themselves for fear,
All the knights at Camelot:
But Lancelot mused a little space;
He said, 'She has a lovely face;
God in his mercy lend her grace,
The Lady of Shalott.'

Alfred, Lord Tennyson

FRUIT AND FLOWERS

This Is Just to Say

This is just to say
I have eaten
the plums
that were in
the icebox

and which
you were probably
saving
for breakfast

Forgive me
they were delicious
so sweet
and so cold

William Carlos Williams

from The Old Wives' Tale

Song
When as the rye reach to the chin,
And chopcherry, chopcherry ripe within,
Strawberries swimming in the cream,
And schoolboys playing in the stream;
Then Oh, then Oh, then Oh, my true-love said,
Till that time come again
She could not live a maid.

George Peele

Given an Apple

He brought her an apple. She would not eat
And he was hurt until she said,
'I'm keeping it as a charm. It may
Grow small and wrinkled. I don't care.
I'll always think of you today.
Time is defeated for that hour
When you gave me an apple for
A love token, and more.'

Elizabeth Jennings

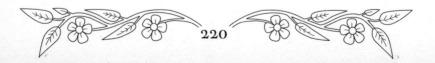

Moonlit Apples

At the top of the house the apples are laid in rows,
And the skylight lets the moonlight in, and those
Apples are deep-sea apples of green. There goes
  A cloud on the moon in the autumn night.

A mouse in the wainscot scratches, and scratches, and then
There is no sound at the top of the house of men
Or mice; and the cloud is blown, and the moon again
  Dapples the apples with deep-sea light.

They are lying in rows there, under the gloomy beams;
On the sagging floor; they gather the silver streams
Out of the moon, those moonlit apples of dreams,
  And quiet is the steep stair under.

In the corridors under there is nothing but sleep.
And stiller than ever on orchard boughs they keep
Tryst with the moon, and deep is the silence, deep
  On moon-washed apples of wonder.

John Drinkwater

Millions of Strawberries

Marcia and I went over the curve,
Eating our way down
Jewels of strawberries we didn't deserve,
Eating our way down.
Till our hands were sticky, and our lips painted.
And over us the hot day fainted,
And we saw snakes
And got scratched
And a lust overcame us for the red unmatched
Small buds of berries,
Till we lay down –
Eating our way down –
And rolled in the berries like two little dogs,
Rolled
In the late gold.
And gnats hummed,
And it was cold,
And home we went, home without a berry,
Painted red and brown
Eating our way down.

Genevieve Taggard

222

from Goblin Market

Morning and evening
Maids heard the goblins cry:
'Come buy our orchard fruits,
Come buy, come buy:
Apples and quinces,
Lemons and oranges,
Plump unpeck'd cherries,
Melons and raspberries,
Bloom-down-cheek'd peaches,
Swart-headed mulberries,
Wild free-born cranberries,
Crab-apples, dewberries,
Pine-apples, blackberries,
Apricots, strawberries; –
All ripe together
In summer weather, –   ➤

Morns that pass by,
Fair eves that fly;
Come buy, come buy:
Our grapes fresh from the vine,
Pomegranates full and fine,
Dates and sharp bullaces,
Rare pears and greengages,
Damsons and bilberries,
Taste them and try:
Currants and gooseberries,
Bright-fire-like barberries,
Figs to fill your mouth,
Citrons from the South,
Sweet to tongue and sound to eye;
Come buy, come buy.'

Christina Rossetti

What Is Pink?

What is pink? A rose is pink
By the fountain's brink.
What is red? A poppy's red
In its barley bed.
What is blue? The sky is blue
Where the clouds float through.
What is white? A swan is white
Sailing in the light.
What is yellow? Pears are yellow,
Rich and ripe and mellow.
What is green? The grass is green,
With small flowers between.
What is violet? Clouds are violet
In the summer twilight.
What is orange? Why, an orange,
Just an orange!

Christina Rossetti

Time of Roses

It was not in the winter
  Our loving lot was cast;
It was the time of roses –
  We plucked them as we passed!

That churlish season never frowned
  On early lovers yet:
O no – the world was newly crowned
  With flowers when first we met!

'Twas twilight, and I bade you go,
  But still you held me fast;
It was the time of roses –
  We plucked them as we passed!

Thomas Hood

Lilies Are White

Lilies are white,
Rosemary's green.
When you are King,
I will be Queen.

Roses are red,
Lavender's blue.
If you will have me,
I will have you.

Anon.

Daffodils

I wander'd lonely as a cloud
 That floats on high o'er vales and hills,
When all at once I saw a crowd,
 A host of golden daffodils;
Beside the lake, beneath the trees,
Fluttering and dancing in the breeze.

Continuous as the stars that shine
 And twinkle on the Milky Way,
They stretch'd in never-ending line
 Along the margin of a bay:
Ten thousand saw I at a glance,
Tossing their heads in sprightly dance.

The waves beside them danced, but they
 Out-did the sparkling waves in glee:
A poet could not but be gay,
 In such a jocund company:
I gazed – and gazed – but little thought
What wealth the show to me had brought:

For oft, when on my couch I lie
 In vacant or in pensive mood,
They flash upon that inward eye
 Which is the bliss of solitude;
And then my heart with pleasure fills,
And dances with the daffodils.

William Wordsworth

Foxgloves

Foxgloves on the moon keep to dark caves.
They come out at the dark of the moon only and in waves
Swarm through the moon-towns and wherever there's a chink
Slip into the houses and spill all the money, clink-clink,
And crumple the notes and re-arrange the silver dishes,
And dip hands into the goldfish bowls and stir the goldfishes,
And thumb the edges of the mirrors, and touch the sleepers
Then at once vanish into the far distance with a wild laugh
　　leaving the house smelling faintly of Virginia Creepers.

Ted Hughes

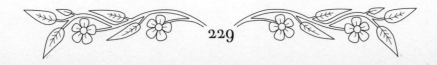

Spring Song
from Love's Labour's Lost

When daisies pied and violets blue
    And lady-smocks all silver white
And cuckoo-buds of yellow hue
    Do paint the meadows with delight,
The cuckoo then, on every tree,
Mocks married men; for thus sings he,
      Cuckoo;
Cuckoo, cuckoo: Oh word of fear,
Unpleasing to a married ear!

When shepherds pipe on oaten straws,
    And merry larks are ploughmen's clocks,
When turtles tread, and rooks, and daws,
    And maidens bleach their summer smocks,
The cuckoo then, on every tree,
Mocks married men; for thus sings he,
      Cuckoo;
Cuckoo, cuckoo: Oh word of fear,
Unpleasing to a married ear!

William Shakespeare

Loveliest of Trees

Loveliest of trees, the cherry now
Is hung with bloom along the bough,
And stands about the woodland ride
Wearing white for Eastertide.

Now, of my threescore years and ten,
Twenty will not come again,
And take from seventy springs a score,
It only leaves me fifty more.

And since to look at things in bloom
Fifty springs are little room,
About the woodlands I will go
To see the cherry hung with snow.

A. E. Housman

Come On into My Tropical Garden

Come on into my tropical garden
Come on in and have a laugh in
Taste my sugar cake and my pine drink
Come on in please come on in

And yes you can stand up in my hammock
and breeze out in my trees
you can pick my hibiscus
and kiss my chimpanzees

O you can roll up in the grass
and if you pick up a flea
I'll take you down for a quick dip-wash
in the sea
believe me there's nothing better
for getting rid of a flea
than having a quick dip-wash in the sea

Come on into my tropical garden
Come on in please come on in

Grace Nichols

Time

'Established' is a good word; much used in garden books,
'The plant, when established'...
Oh, become established quickly, quickly, garden!
For I am fugitive, I am very fugitive –

Those that come after me will gather these roses,
And watch, as I do now, the white wistaria
Burst, in the sunshine, from its pale green sheath.

Planned. Planted. Established. Then neglected,
Till at last the loiterer by the gate will wonder
At the old, old cottage, the old wooden cottage,
And say, 'One might build here, the view is glorious;
This must have been a pretty garden once.'

Mary Ursula Bethell

PLACES

I Remember, I Remember

I remember, I remember
The house where I was born,
The little window where the sun
Came peeping in at morn;
He never came a wink too soon,
Nor brought too long a day,
But now, I often wish the night
Had borne my breath away!

I remember, I remember
The roses, red and white,
The violets, and the lily-cups,
Those flowers made of light!
The lilacs where the robin built,
And where my brother set
The laburnum on his birthday, –
The tree is living yet!

I remember, I remember
Where I was used to swing,
And thought the air must rush as fresh
To swallows on the wing;
My spirit flew in feathers then,
That is so heavy now,
And summer pools could hardly cool
The fever on my brow!

I remember, I remember
The fir-trees dark and high;
I used to think their slender tops
Were close against the sky:
It was a childish ignorance,
But now 'tis little joy
To know I'm farther off from heav'n
Than when I was a boy.

Thomas Hood

Cottage

When I live in a Cottage
I shall keep in my Cottage
  Two different Dogs
  Three creamy Cows
  Four giddy Goats
  Five pewter Pots
  Six silver Spoons
  Seven busy Beehives
  Eight ancient Appletrees
  Nine red Rosebushes
  Ten teeming Teapots
  Eleven chirping Chickens
  Twelve cosy Cats with their kittenish Kittens
      and
  One blessèd Baby in a Basket.
That's what I'll have when I live in my Cottage.

Eleanor Farjeon

The Lake Isle of Innisfree

I will arise and go now, and go to Innisfree,
And a small cabin build there, of clay and wattles made:
Nine bean-rows will I have there, a hive for the honey-bee,
And live alone in the bee-loud glade.

And I shall have some peace there, for peace comes
   dropping slow,
Dropping from the veils of the morningto where the
   cricket sings;
There midnight's all a glimmer, and noon a purple glow,
And evening full of the linnet's wings.

I will arise and go now, for always night and day
I hear lake water lapping with low sounds by the shore;
While I stand on the roadway, or on the pavements grey,
I hear it in the deep heart's core.

W. B. Yeats

Stopping by Woods on a Snowy Evening

Whose woods these are I think I know.
His house is in the village though;
He will not see me stopping here
To watch his woods fill up with snow.

My little horse must think it queer
To stop without a farmhouse near
Between the woods and frozen lake
The darkest evening of the year.

He gives his harness bells a shake
To ask if there is some mistake.
The only other sound's the sweep
Of easy wind and downy flake.

The woods are lovely, dark and deep.
But I have promises to keep,
And miles to go before I sleep,
And miles to go before I sleep.

Robert Frost

The Way through the Woods

They shut the road through the woods
Seventy years ago.
Weather and rain have undone it again,
And now you would never know
There was once a road through the woods
Before they planted the trees.
It is underneath the coppice and heath,
And the thin anemones.
Only the keeper sees
That, where the ring-dove broods,
And the badgers roll at ease,
There was once a road through the woods.

Yet, if you enter the woods
Of a summer evening late,
When the night-air cools on the trout-ringed pools
Where the otter whistles his mate,
(They fear not men in the woods,
Because they see so few.)
You will hear the beat of a horse's feet,
And the swish of a skirt in the dew,
Steadily cantering through
The misty solitudes,
As though they perfectly knew
The old lost road through the woods ...
But there is no road through the woods.

Rudyard Kipling

Adlestrop

Yes. I remember Adlestrop –
The name, because one afternoon
Of heat the express-train drew up there
Unwontedly. It was late June.

The steam hissed. Someone cleared his throat.
No one left and no one came
On the bare platform. What I saw
Was Adlestrop – only the name

And willows, willow-herb, and grass,
And meadowsweet, and haycocks dry,
No whit less still and lonely fair
Than the high cloudlets in the sky.

And for that minute a blackbird sang
Close by, and round him, mistier,
Farther and farther, all the birds
Of Oxfordshire and Gloucestershire.

Edward Thomas

The Counties

Saturday 7 August 2010
(It was announced that county names could disappear by
2016 after Royal Mail unveiled plans to delete them from its
database)

But I want to write to an Essex girl,
greeting her warmly.
But I want to write to a Shropshire lad,
brave boy, home from the army,
and I want to write to the Lincolnshire Poacher
to hear of his hare
and to an aunt in Bedfordshire
who makes a wooden hill of her stair.
But I want to post a rose to a Lancashire lass,
red, I'll pick it,
and I want to write to a Middlesex mate
for tickets for cricket.
But I want to write to the Ayrshire cheesemaker
and his good cow
and it is my duty to write to the Queen at Berkshire
in praise of Slough.
But I want to write to the National Poet of Wales at Ceredigion
in celebration
and I want to write to the Dorset Giant
in admiration
and I want to write to a widow in Rutland
in commiseration
and to the Inland Revenue in Yorkshire
in desperation. ⇝➤

But I want to write to my uncle in Clackmannanshire
in his kilt
and to my scrumptious cousin in Somerset
with her cidery lilt.
But I want to write to two ladies in Denbighshire,
near Llangollen
and I want to write to a laddie in Lanarkshire,
Dear Lachlan . . .
But I want to write to the Cheshire Cat,
returning its smile.
But I want to write the names of the Counties down
for my own child
and may they never be lost to her . . .
all the birds of Oxfordshire and Gloucestershire . . .

Carol Ann Duffy

RAINBOWS,
MOONS AND STARS

Spell to Bring a Smile

Come down Rainbow
Rainbow come down

I have a space for you
in my small face

If my face is too small for you
take a space in my chest

If my chest is too small for you
take a space in my belly

If my belly is too small for you
then take every part of me

Come down Rainbow
Rainbow come down

You can eat me from head to toe

John Agard

My Heart Leaps Up

My heart leaps up when I behold
    A rainbow in the sky:
So was it when my life began;
So is it now I am a man;
So be it when I shall grow old,
    Or let me die!
The Child is father of the Man;
And I could wish my days to be
Bound each to each by natural piety.

William Wordsworth

Above the Dock

Above the quiet dock in midnight,
Tangled in the tall mast's corded height,
Hangs the moon. What seemed so far away
is but a child's balloon, forgotten after play.

T. E. Hulme

Lemon Moon

On a hot and thirsty summer night,
The moon's a wedge of lemon light
Sitting low among the trees,
Close enough for you to squeeze
And make a moonade, icy-sweet,
To cool your summer-dusty heat.

Beverly McLoughland

The Moon Landing
July 1969

To celebrate
the first moonwalk
I invented
my own TV

All it took
was a cardboard box
some bottle tops
a spot of glue
and a piece of card –
on which I drew
an orange moon
with a tiny astronaut man
on top

Nearly everyone
came round
our house
on the big day

And the whole world
seemed to stop breathing
for a moment
as we watched
those fuzzy pictures
and listened
to those crackly voices
travelling thousands
of miles
from the moon
into our home

In fact
my aunty
reckoned my TV
was even better
than watching
the real thing –
so she put it
in the window
so everyone passing
could see
my paper moon

James Carter

Where Am I?

There are mountains here, and craters,
and places with beautiful names:
The Bay of Rainbows,
The Lake of Dreams,
The Sea of Nectar,
The Sea of Tranquillity.
There is no water
in the seas or the lakes.

The hottest days
are hotter than boiling water.
The nights are colder
than anywhere on Earth.

I can see stars very clearly,
and nearer than them,
something wonderful. Imagine
a huge blue and white marble
glowing in a black sky.

Wendy Cope

The Heavenly City

I sigh for the heavenly country,
Where the heavenly people pass,
And the sea is as quiet as a mirror
Of beautiful, beautiful glass.

I walk in the heavenly field,
With lilies and poppies bright,
I am dressed in a heavenly coat
Of polished white.

When I walk in the heavenly parkland
My feet on the pastures are bare,
Tall waves the grass, but no harmful
Creature is there.

At night I fly over the housetops,
And stand on the bright moony beams;
Gold are all heaven's rivers,
And silver her streams.

Stevie Smith

The More Loving One

Looking up at the stars, I know quite well
That, for all they care, I can go to hell,
But on earth indifference is the least
We have to dread from man or beast.

How should we like it were stars to burn
With a passion for us we could not return?
If equal affection cannot be,
Let the more loving one be me.

Admirer as I think I am
Of stars that do not give a damn,
I cannot, how I see them, say
I missed one terribly all day.

Were all stars to disappear or die,
I should learn to look at an empty sky
And feel its total dark sublime,
Though this might take me a little time.

W. H. Auden

When I Heard the Learn'd Astronomer

When I heard the learn'd astronomer,
When the proofs, the figures, were ranged in columns before
    me,
When I was shown the charts and diagrams, to add, divide, and
    measure them,
When I sitting heard the astronomer where he lectured with
    much applause in the lecture-room,
How soon unaccountable I became tired and sick,
Till rising and gliding out I wander'd off by myself,
In the mystical moist night-air, and from time to time,
Look'd up in perfect silence at the stars.

Walt Whitman

Index of First Lines

A fairy went a-marketing   51
Above the quiet dock in midnight   248
And staying inside the lines   153
Annabel-Emily Huntington-Horne   164
As I walked out one evening   196
At the top of the house the apples are laid in rows   221
Aunt Jennifer's tigers prance across a screen   30
Break, break, break   134
But I want to write to an Essex girl   243
Children born of fairy stock   53
Clownlike, happiest on your hands   126
Come down Rainbow   246
Come live with me and be my Love   188
Come on into my tropical garden   232
Dad keeps Mum's favourite dress   28
Dear God   74
Dear Grandmamma, with what we give   34
Dear Mum   25
Do I love you   189
Do you remember an Inn   161
Don't bite your nails, Amanda!   154
'Established' is a good word; much used in garden books   233
Everyone grumbled. The sky was grey   29
Fear no more the heat o' the sun   132
February 14th   175
Fly away, fly away, over the sea   76
For I will consider my cat Jeoffry   85

For months he taught us, stiff-faced   119

Foxgloves on the moon keep to dark caves   229

Full fathom five thy father lies   135

Fur is soft, skin isn't   94

Give yourself a hug   15

Good girls   158

Grandad used to be a pop star   38

Granny Granny please comb my hair   33

Half-hidden in a graveyard   136

He brought her an apple. She would not eat   220

He was seven and I was six, my Brendon Gallacher   150

Her day out from the workhouse-ward, she stands   166

How do I love thee? Let me count the ways   190

I am a witch, and a kind old witch   58

I can remember. I can remember   142

I fear it's very wrong of me   5

I heard you were coming and   174

I must not think of thee; and, tired yet strong   194

I remember, I remember   236

I sigh for the heavenly country   253

I took her for my kind of person   6

I wander'd lonely as a cloud   228

I was as good as gold, an angel, said ta very much,
    no thanks   156

I was best friends with Sabah   13

I was writing my doll's name on the back of her neck   27

I went out to the hazel wood   204

I went to school   110

I will arise and go now, and go to Innisfree   239

I will make you brooches and toys for your delight   173

If no one ever marries me, –   152
I'm nobody! Who are you?   14
I'm not   140
In among the silver birches   183
In Art I drew a park   106
Isabel met an enormous bear   145
It was a little captive cat   80
It was not in the winter   226
I've found a small dragon in the woodshed   92
Jellicle Cats come out tonight   81
Just off the highway to Rochester, Minnesota   91
Leaping and dancing   181
Lilies are white   227
Looking up at the stars, I know quite well   254
Love set you going like a fat gold watch   127
Loveliest of trees, the cherry now   231
maggie and milly and molly and may   148
Marcia and I went over the curve   222
Me and my best pal (well, she was   8
Minnie and Winnie   160
Morning and evening   223
Mother, I love you so   24
Mother said if I wore this hat   66
Mrs Mackenzie's quite stern   109
Mum and me had a row yesterday   67
my auntie gives me a colouring book and crayons   31
My baby brother makes so much noise   19
My friend   11
My heart is like a singing bird   186
My heart leaps up when I behold   247

My team   104
My turn for Audrey Pomegranate   4
No one makes soup like my Grandpa's   40
Nobody heard him, the dead man   129
Now sleeps the crimson petal, now the white   187
Nuns, now: ladies in black hoods   99
Nymph, nymph, what are your beads?   42
O lovely O most charming pug   88
'O what can ail thee, Knight-at-arms   202
Of all the girls that are so smart   191
Oh I'm in love with the janitor's boy   172
On a hot and thirsty summer night   249
On either side the river lie   210
On the first day of Christmas   177
Our teacher's pet   102
Over hill, over dale   54
Prior Knowledge was a strange boy   7
Remember me when I am gone away   131
Remember, remember, there's many a thing   36
Round about the cauldron go   60
Sabrina fair   45
Saris hang on the washing line   64
See, they are clearing the sawdust course   149
Seventeen years ago you said   195
Shall I compare thee to a summer's day?   199
She starts   with red   65
She went, to plain-work, and to purling brooks   163
She wished she could fly   48
Since Christmas they have lived with us   21
Sitting on the stairs   182

Sleep, baby, sleep	18
Stop all the clocks, cut off the telephone	133
The cat went here and there	83
The Cow comes home swinging	90
The fairy child loved her spider	50
The friendly cow, all red and white	89
The long-legged girl who takes goal-kicks is me	2
The new girl stood at Miss Moon's desk	107
The Owl and the Pussy-cat went to sea	77
The wind sings its gusty song	114
There are mountains here, and craters	252
There, in a meadow, by the river's side	44
There once was a frog	79
There was a naughty boy	138
There was an old woman named Towl	167
There was once a line	100
They shut the road through the woods	241
They went to sea in a Sieve, they did	205
This is just to say	218
Though she doesn't know it	117
Three Turkeys fair their last have breathed	75
Thrice toss these oaken ashes in the air	57
To celebrate	250
Today we went out of school	113
Two cats	84
Tyger! Tyger! burning bright	87
Uncle Edward was colour-blind	32
Up the airy mountain	55
Way down Geneva	69
We are the Workhouse children	208

'We did sums at school, Mummy –   98

Welcome to St Judas   121

We've been at the seaside all day   115

What is pink? A rose is pink   225

What with getting in the way of the packing   128

When as the rye reach to the chin   219

When daisies pied and violets blue   230

When Grandmamma fell off the boat   35

When I am an old woman I shall wear purple   71

When I am dead, my dearest   130

When I come home from school he doesn't bark   93

When I come out of the bathroom   96

When I heard the learn'd astronomer   255

When I live in a Cottage   238

When my baby brother   20

When my friend Anita runs   10

When you teach me   120

Where can I find seven small girls to be pets   61

Who would be *(A merman bold)*   47

Who would be *(A mermaid fair)*   46

Whose woods these are I think I know   240

Wings whispered about her hair   49

Yes. I remember Adlestrop –   242

You live in the hollow of a stranded whale   23

Index of Poets

Adcock, Fleur   4, 27, 98, 99, 128

Agard, John   246

Ahlberg, Allan   11

Allingham, William   55

Alma-Tadema, Laurence   152

Anon.   18, 167, 177, 227

Ardagh, Philip   121

Auden, W. H.   133, 196, 254

Barrett Browning,
    Elizabeth   190

Belloc, Hilaire   34, 161

Bernos de Gasztold,
    Carmen   74

Bethell, Mary Ursula   233

Betjeman, John   183

Bevan, Clare   25, 50, 107

Blake, William   87

Calder, Dave   119

Campion, Thomas   57

Carey, Henry   191

Carter, James   189, 250

Causley, Charles   164, 208

Chatterjee, Debjani   64

Coe, Mandy   2, 28, 48

Coelho, Joseph   106

Cope, Wendy   6, 252

Cornford, Frances   58

Coward, Noel   142

Crane, Nathalia   172

Cummings, E. E.   148

De la Mare, Walter   136

Dean, Jan   153

Dickinson, Emily   14

Drinkwater, John   221

Duffy, Carol Ann   7, 36, 38, 61, 93, 120, 156, 243

Elliot, T. S.   81

Fanthorpe, U. A.   94, 181

Farjeon, Eleanor   238

Field, Rachel   149

Fleming, Marjory   75, 88

Floyd, Gillian   109

Foster, John   20, 102

Frost, Robert   240

Fyleman, Rose   51

Geras, Adèle   65

Gibson, Wilfrid   166

Godden, Rumer, tr.   74

Graham, Harry   35

Graves, Robert   53

Green, Mary   117

Harmer, David   115

Hegley, John   31

Henri, Adrian   140, 182

Hood, Thomas   226, 236

Housman, A. E. 231
Hughes, Ted 90, 229
Hulme, T. E. 248
Jennings, Elizabeth 5, 220
Joseph, Jenny 71, 174
Kay, Jackie 8, 13, 19, 40, 79, 150
Keats, John 138, 202
Kipling, Rudyard 241
Klein, Robin 154
Lear, Edward 77, 205
McLoughland, Beverly 249
Magee, Wes 110
Marlowe, Christopher 188
Mew, Charlotte 195
Meynell, Alice 194
Milne, Ewart 84
Milton, John 45
Monro, Harold 42
Morgan, Michaela 175
Nagle, Frances 104
Nash, Ogden 145
Nichols, Grace 10, 15, 33, 232
Noyes, Alfred 29
O'Callaghan, Julie 23
Parelkar, Ruhee 100
Patten, Brian 92
Peele, George 219
Plath, Sylvia 21, 126, 127
Pope, Alexander 163
Rawnsley, Irene 67, 158

Rice, John 114
Rich, Adrienne 30
Rossetti, Christina 76, 130, 131, 186, 223, 225
Scannell, Vernon 32
Shakespeare, William 54, 60, 132, 135, 199, 230
Smart, Christopher 85
Smith, Stevie 24, 66, 80, 129, 253
Spenser, Edmund 44
Stevenson, Robert Louis 89, 173
Swinger, Marian 49
Taggard, Genevieve 222
Tennyson, Alfred, Lord 46, 47, 134, 160, 187, 210
Thesen, Sharon 96
Thomas, Edward 242
Whitehead, David 113
Whitman, Walt 255
Williams, William Carlos 218
Wordsworth, William 228, 247
Wright, James 91
Wright, Kit 69
Yeats, W. B. 83, 204, 239

Acknowledgements

The compiler and publisher would like to thank the following for permission to use copyright material:

Fleur Adcock, 'Tunbridge Wells', 'Sidcup, 1940', 'Halfway Street, Sidcup', 'St Gertrude's, Sidcup' and 'Drury Goodbyes' all from *Poems 1960–2000* (Bloodaxe Books, 2000); John Agard, 'Spell to Bring a Smile' copyright © John Agard; Allan Ahlberg, 'It Is a Puzzle', by permission of the Penguin Group Ltd; Philip Ardagh, 'St Judas Welcomes Author Philip Arder', by permission of the author; W. H. Auden, 'Stop All the Clocks' and 'The More Loving One' from *Collected Works*, copyright © 1976, 1991, the Estate of W. H. Auden; Hilaire Belloc, 'Grandmamma's Birthday' and 'Tarantella' from *Complete Verse* by Hilaire Belloc (copyright © Hilaire Belloc is reproduced by permission of PFD [www.pfd.co.uk] on behalf of Hilaire Belloc); Carmen Bernos de Gasztold, 'The Prayer of the Little Ducks' from *Prayers from the Ark*, trans. Rumer Godden, 1963, by permission of Macmillan Children's Books; Claire Bevan, 'The Housemaid's Letter' from *The Works 2*, ed. Brian Moses and Pie Corbett, Macmillan Children's Books (2002), by permission of the author; 'The Spider' from *Fairy Poems*, Macmillan Children's Books (2004), by permission of the author; 'The New Girl' from *Spooky Schools*, ed. Brian Moses, Macmillan Children's Books (2004), by permission of the author; Dave Calder, 'Changed' from *Dolphins Leap Lampposts*, Macmillan Children's Books (2002), by permission of the author; James Carter, 'Love You More' from *Time-Travelling Underpants*, Macmillan Children's Books (2007), by permission of the author; 'The Moon Landing' from *Greetings, Earthlings!* by Brian Moses and James Carter, Macmillan Children's Books (2009), by permission of the author; Charles Causley, 'Annabel-Emily' and 'On St Catherine's Day' from I *Had a Little Cat*, Macmillan Children's Books (2009); Debjani Chatterjee, 'My Sari' is reprinted from *Unzip Your Lips: 100 Poems to Read Aloud*, Macmillan Children's Books (1998), copyright © Dr Debjani Chatterjee 1998, reprinted by permission of the author; Mandy Coe, 'Me & You' from *Read Me*, chosen by Gaby Morgan, Macmillan Children's Books (2004), by permission of the author; 'Sensing Mother' from *Sensational!*, chosen by Roger McGough, Macmillan Children's Books (2004), by permission of the author; 'Wish' from *Fairy Poems*, chosen by Gaby Morgan, Macmillan Children's Books (2006), by permission of the author;

Joseph Coelho, 'Make It Bigger, Eileen!', by permission of the author; Wendy Cope, 'Sporty People' and 'Where Am I?' published by Faber and Faber Ltd; Frances Cornford, 'The Old Witch in the Copse', by kind permission of the Trustees of the Mrs Frances Crofts Cornford Will Trust; Noel Coward, 'The Boy Actor', copyright © Oxford University Press; E. E. Cummings, 'maggie and milly and molly and may' copyright © 1956, 1984, 1991 by the Trustees for the E. E. Cummings Trust; Walter de la Mare, 'The Stranger', The Literary Trustees of Walter de la Mare and The Society of Authors as their representative; Jan Dean, 'Colouring In' first published in *Mice on Ice*, ed. Gaby Morgan, Macmillan Children's Books (2004); John Drinkwater, 'Moonlit Apples' from *Collected Poems*, 1923 – reprinted by permission of Pan Macmillan; Carol Ann Duffy, 'Prior Knowledge', 'Your Grandmother', 'The Giantess', 'Toy Dog', 'Teacher' and 'Halo' all published by Faber and Faber Ltd; 'Rooty Tooty' and 'The Counties', by permission of Rogers, Coleridge and White Ltd; T. S. Elliot, 'The Song of the Jellicles' published by Faber and Faber Ltd; U. A. Fanthorpe, 'Dear True Love', from U. A. Fanthorpe *New and Collected Poems*, Enitharmon Press, 2010, with acknowledgement to Dr R.V. Bailey; Eleanor Farjeon, 'Cottage' from *Then There Were Three* published by Michael Joseph by permission of David Higham Associates Ltd; Gillian Floyd, 'Mrs Mackenzie', by permission of the author; John Foster, 'My Baby Brother's Secrets' and 'Inside Sir's Matchbox', both by permission of the author; Robert Frost, 'Stopping by Woods on a Snowy Evening' from *The Poetry of Robert Frost* edited by Edward Connery Latham, published by Johnathan Cape, reprinted by permission of The Random House Group Ltd and Henry Holt and Company; Rose Fyleman, 'A Fairy Went a-Marketing', by permission of The Society of Authors; Adèle Geras, 'Patchwork', by permission of the author; Wilfrid Gibson, 'The Ice', by permission of Pan Macmillan; Robert Graves, 'I'd Love to Be a Fairy's Child', by permission of A. P. Watt Ltd on behalf of The Trustees of the Robert Graves Copyright Trust; Mary Green, 'Ms Fleur' first published in *When Teacher Isn't Looking*, poems chosen by David Harmer, Macmillan Children's Books (2001); David Harmer, 'We Lost Our Teacher to the Sea', copyright © David Harmer; John Hegley, 'Uncle and Auntie' by permission of Carlton Books and Peters, Fraser & Dunlop; Adrian Henri, 'What Are Little Girls . . .' and 'Party' published in *Not Fade Away* (Bloodaxe Books 1994), copyright © Rogers, Coleridge and White Ltd; Ted Hughes, 'Cow' and 'Foxgloves' published by Faber and Faber Ltd; Elizabeth Jennings, 'Friends' and Given an Apple' from *A Secret*

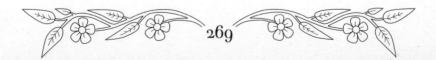